# LEADERSHIP LESSONS
# FOR HEALTH CARE PROVIDERS

# LEADERSHIP LESSONS FOR HEALTH CARE PROVIDERS

FRANK J. LEXA, MD, MBA

*Chair, American College of Radiology Commission on Leadership
and Practice Development and Chief Medical Officer,
the Radiology Leadership Institute of the ACR & Project Faculty,
Spain and East Asia Regional Manager, the Global Consulting
Practicum and Professor (adj.) of Marketing, The Wharton School,
University of Pennsylvania Philadelphia, PA, United States*

ELSEVIER

AMSTERDAM • BOSTON • HEIDELBERG • LONDON
NEW YORK • OXFORD • PARIS • SAN DIEGO
SAN FRANCISCO • SINGAPORE • SYDNEY • TOKYO

Academic Press is an imprint of Elsevier

**Library of Congress Cataloging-in-Publication Data**
A catalog record for this book is available from the Library of Congress

**British Library Cataloguing-in-Publication Data**
A catalogue record for this book is available from the British Library

ISBN: 978-0-12-801866-8

For information on all Academic Press publications
visit our website at https://www.elsevier.com/

  Working together
to grow libraries in
Book Aid
International developing countries

www.elsevier.com • www.bookaid.org

*Publisher:* Sara Tenney
*Acquisition Editor:* Mary Preap
*Editorial Project Manager:* Joslyn Chaiprasert-Paguio
*Production Project Manager:* Lucía Pérez
*Designer:* Mark Rogers

Typeset by Thomson Digital

*Dedicated to all of the leaders in medicine
who have brought out the best in those
who devote their lives to the healing arts
and to all the leaders to come*

# Contents

## 16. Leadership in Conflict

## 17. Leading in a Crisis

## 18. Tough Choices: How Leaders Make the Hard Decisions

## 19. Leadership and Mistakes

## 20. Thinking About Failures in Leadership

## 21. Becoming a Level 5 Leader

## 22. Choosing Greatness in Leadership

## 23. Winning in a Crisis

## 24. Leading in Serious Conflicts

## 25. Leadership and Trust

## 26. Principled Leadership

## 27. Motivation and Leadership

## 28. Succession Leadership

## 29. Leadership: The Last 100 Days

## 30. Conclusions and Next Steps

# Acknowledgments

There are far too many people who deserve acknowledgments for their contributions to this book and I apologize in advance for not being able to name everyone in this space. I do need to start by thanking Dr. Bruce Hillman, the editor of the *Journal of the American College of Radiology*, first for his suggestion that I do the project that grew into the leadership columns in that August journal, and second for his continuing support for this endeavor over the years as it has grown into book form.

In the history of ideas and inventions, it is remarkable how often the important innovations have resulted more from the interactions between people than from individuals (see Shenk, 2014). I have been fortunate in my career to work with many people who have helped me in understanding both the need for leadership and the nature of good leadership. There are both opportunities and perils at the interface between medicine and the world of business. I have had the experience of being creatively paired myself with such luminaries of the American College of Radiology as Drs. Larry Muroff, Jonathan Berlin, Richard Duszak, Geraldine McGinty, Alex Norbash, Giles Boland, Bibb Allen, Bill Thorwarth, Paul Ellenbogen, John Patti, Jim Thrall, Jim Brink, Van Moore, Michael Bruno, and many others.

I have also had the opportunity to collaborate and work with many rising stars in radiology who have already contributed greatly to many facets of medical leadership including: Dan Mollura, James Y. Chen, Matt Hawkins, and Jonathan Flug.

From my two stints of duty at University of Pennsylvania School of Medicine (now the Perelman School), I had the good fortune to work with luminary neuroradiologists such as Scott Atlas, David Yousem, David Hackney, Elias Melhem, and Robert Grossman, who have all gone on to become great leaders in radiology and in some cases beyond. Dr. Bruce Kneeland deserves special mention for encouraging me to give academic medicine a second chance and for showing how leadership can succeed despite serious challenges.

At Wharton, we teach leadership itself and we strive to train people in the disciplines that are critical for mastering leadership. Over the past 19 years, I have worked on over a 100 projects in one way or another with our faculty student teams in both the graduate and executive programs. I have lost track of how many countries we have been to, but the work has taken me to five continents so far and I have assisted on work that was ongoing on the sixth (nothing in Antarctica on the horizon).

Along the way, we have always come back to the notion of how we can effectively train people to be more successful in their careers and how important leadership is to our students. We try to have them learn by doing. They learn to lead their student groups as well as working with a team of overseas students. We teach them leadership by having them take the lead on project management, on strategic thinking, and on client management. From the beginning, Len Lodish has been an inspiring mentor and along the way, I have learned a great deal from my colleagues, especially Rob Mann, Jeff Babin, and Steve Smolinsky.

One of the themes of this book will be the universality of leadership—it is of course neither limited to my speciality, nor to healthcare. Without naming names, the many brilliant and fascinating people who made up "the 14" in Cambridge and later the Cowper Street gang in Palo Alto have my gratitude for the inspiration that led to this project.

Finally to my family, my thanks for their understanding and help as I wrote this book: especially Alek and Matthew for putting up with the time I spent on this and my muse, Tanya for helping turn my ideas into prose. Thanks!

*Image credit: Effigy of Richard I of England in the church of Fontevraud Abbey; Wikimedia Commons*

# Introduction

"Uneasy lies the head that wears a crown"
—*William Shakespeare in "Henry IV – Part II" (1597), 1564–1616*

"It's good to be the king"
—*Mel Brooks in "History of the World, Part I" (1981), 1936-present*

This book grew out of a series of leadership columns that I wrote for the *Journal of the American College of Radiology (JACR)* from 2008 to 2013. This initial small experiment eventually grew to a total of 25 installments introducing and exploring the issues that medical leaders face. The topics ranged from how to prepare to be a leader, to what you should do first when you take the reins, all the way to how to gracefully step down and move on in your career and your life. They were short and focused both by design and also by necessity. I wrote them for an audience which is predominately US-based physicians in the specialty of radiology, but as nonradiologists looked at them an interesting thing occurred. I was told by friends who are in other medical specialties, as well as people who were in nursing, who were in dentistry, and in some additional fields that the advice was also applicable in their professions. Moreover, they asked if I knew of a good book for people like them (and me) for aspiring healthcare leaders. That was the moment when I had the thought of writing a user friendly book that they could use to get started in leadership and then have as a handy reference when the need arises during leadership challenges.

The focus both of those columns and of this book is on those medical and scientific people who need to learn more about leadership as they progress in their careers, but who don't have time now—and haven't had the time in the past to take time out from their career and pursue a degree or a program that includes dedicated leadership training. An apt title for this book could also have been "Leadership for busy professionals." Many of the people who need to know more about leadership are also those who are so immersed in their day jobs that they don't have the time nor do they have the opportunity to take time off and obtain formal leadership training. They face the conundrum of needing a leadership education but the needs of their day jobs, the demands of family, and sometimes the economic realities of their work preclude taking time off to go back to school. If you have felt this way during your career, then this book can help you with getting started on the path toward leadership.

This book is based upon my own career in medicine but I have also drawn on my experiences from the work that I have been doing outside of medicine: in strategic consulting, entrepreneurship, and venture capital. However, be forewarned (and probably relieved!) this is not a business biography. It is not a 100 pages of the twilight reflections of a retired CEO or general or chairman, reviewing how things were done back in the day. Those are interesting, but the insights that they share rarely are directly on point for those of us in a very different arena in a different time. Rather this tome is a series of lessons, discussions, and references that will hopefully help you to become a leader today. If your work in leadership has already begun, then it can aid you in becoming a better leader in your current position and/or help you as your responsibilities increase. To the extent that I have put my own experiences in here it is to help you avoid mistakes and get things right quickly. I will share not only my successes, but also some of my misses as well. As one of my flight instructors liked to say—usually when we were flying almost upside down over central New Jersey—it is better to learn from other people's mistakes than to make them yourself. I hope though that the lessons here will give you a foundation to help you even though your circumstances, your practice, your hospital, and your times will be at least slightly different than mine.

By way of a brief introduction, I am a practicing physician, specializing in diagnostic radiology and working in the subspecialty of neuroradiology. I work predominately on the diagnostic side, interpreting MRI and CT of the brain and spinal cord. I am involved in taking care of patients with many of the highest impact diseases that afflict our society in the 21st century including stroke, dementia, spinal cord injuries, cancer, demyelinating diseases, etc. I have had the chance to work under many great medical professionals, as well as some who were not so great and also, (probably not surprisingly to anyone who is also in healthcare) occasionally with downright poor medical leaders. One of my observations that I pass along to younger physicians is that I have learned from everyone on that list—sometimes I have learned what to do and at other times I have learned the tough, but important lessons in what *not* to do when you are a healthcare leader.

Those experiences have driven much of the work that led to this book, but it is only half the story. As I noted in the foreword, in another life, I have been teaching at several business schools since 2001, the largest shares are (1) as an adjunct professor at the Wharton School of the University of Pennsylvania and (2) at one of the top European business schools, the Instituto de Empresa in Madrid. My time at the Wharton campuses in Philadelphia and San Francisco has taught me many things about how leaders are made. One of the most surprising is that anyone (almost anyone anyway…) can learn to become a leader. This is an interesting and important notion—just about anyone who is reading this book can learn to become a leader. The only proviso that I would add to that statement is that the individual needs to want to become a leader. Someone who genuinely doesn't want to take on a leadership role can't be forced into a position and then become a great leader. I have seen that mistake now in several institutions. Leaders do need to believe in themselves and have a desire to contribute to their group or department. Without that drive, leaders will just go through the motions and will very likely fail.

A second theme that will run through this book is that every medical leader (no qualification required here) can learn to be better at the job of leading in their institutions. The best leaders already know that. Like being a pilot or becoming a skier or a musician, there are always going to be opportunities to challenge yourself to get better. No one is perfect in their leadership work and you will never run out of things to learn. I will not only pass along that insight, but more importantly will also provide you with advice about how to keep moving forward as you master the lessons in this book and move further along the road of leadership.

As the contrast between the opening quotations at the top of the introduction highlights, we often have more than a little ambivalence when it comes to leadership. As much as we crave the guidance of good leaders, we can also be quite hard on them. This may be found in many aspects of our society, but it is often particularly acute in the field of medicine. Those of us who are trained in the healing arts—physicians, nurses, dentists, pharmacists, nurse practioners, physician assistants, technologists, and the many other—too many to list—categories of those who dedicate their lives to curing disease, alleviating discomfort and promoting good health—often focus our energies primarily on our individual skills and our crafts rather than on the tasks and training that it takes to lead our groups or to take charge in our institutions. Our lack of attention to leadership may make us devalue or distrust those who do.

In addition to inattention to leadership in our careers, there are other impediments that may keep a top nurse or surgeon from developing his or her leadership skills. Negative attitudes toward leaders in hospitals and academic departments are not uncommon and are often compounded by subtle (or fairly overt) snobbery from the medical professionals. There is a tendency to look down on those who have to "count the beans", that is, the "bureaucrats" who keep things running in our institutions and the business professionals who manage the organizational side of healthcare delivery. Healthcare professionals may not value the skills of those who are not in the medical arena and may feel that the perception is mutual.

The gulf is further exacerbated by pervasive deficiencies in or even a basic absence of leadership education in many sectors of healthcare education and training. In many other important fields in our society, for example in the military and in parts of the business and nonprofit sectors, leadership training and development is deeply integrated into the institutional culture. It is part of the training and the work you do, rather than something separated from your educational and vocational activities.

While there are of course exceptions on the medical side, many medical professionals often get to the middle of their career with little or no substantial training in how to lead others or how to manage in medicine. That statement is all the more astounding to nonhealthcare professionals, given the long and arduous years that it takes to finish training in many parts of healthcare. With all that time, it surprises my colleagues in the military and business world that there isn't much in the way of leadership training.

For some medical professionals, the amount of required post college education and training can easily surpass a decade, and yet despite that lengthy process, leadership training is often scant, shallow, or conspicuously absent. The paradox that I see is that leadership skills can help you in your career regardless of your setting and also regardless of whether you are the leader or not. Whether you are in solo practice, a small group or a large hospital chain, leadership skills will be important to you in both personal growth and in developing your career, bringing both to their maximal potentials.

When I put this book together I knew that I couldn't cover every single facet of leadership, let alone every academic debate over the nuances of good and bad leadership in a format of this length. Instead, I wanted to get in enough information to get you started on the trip. Since it is beyond the scope and scale of this volume, I have included reference material for those who want to go deeper into the academic analysis and debates on leadership. Instead in this volume I am trying to get you enough to get you started on your journey and to guide you through the major milestones.

When I was a senior in college, I had still never traveled outside of North America. My graduation present was a round trip coach ticket from JFK to London and what my parents thought was enough money for a backpacking trip of 8 weeks in Europe. I picked up a guide from a college publisher that had enough information for a novice like me to travel through over a dozen countries on a shoestring budget and have the experience of a lifetime. The book didn't cover every place I went, nor did it predict every adventure and misadventure that I ended up having. It did however inspire me to go to Europe instead of spending the summer lifeguarding near my parent's home in Pennsylvania and it also succeeded in getting me through the trip safely and guided me to finding interesting people and places along the way.

My hope is that this book can play a similar role for you. Here I have included references that allow you to go deeper into the topics as well as suggestions for how to continue once our pages together are over. No book of this size can address everything that you will encounter during your adventures in leadership. In this volume, we will discuss how to get started, how to avoid major mistakes, and where the next logical steps in the journey will take you. If that appeals to you, then this is your book.

*Image credit: Illustration of human evolution ending with smart phone. © Frank Fiedler/Shutterstock*

# 1

# Leadership and its Challenges

*"The task of the leader is to get his people from where they are to where they have not been"*
—**Henry A. Kissinger, political scientist, 1923-present**

## LEADERSHIP IN TIME

When we think of leadership, it often invokes a mental image of a highly visible successful alpha individual in government, the military, business, or sports. In some sense at least, leadership is a widely distributed behavioral trait present in a broad variety of pack and herd species beyond just *Homo sapiens*. In fact, some important facets of primate leadership were probably already quite ancient when a great leader or leaders led the first modern humans out of Africa on an expedition that has gone on to encompass the globe. The idea of leadership as a journey and an effort to overcome challenges is still important today. Except for some rare instances where a hospital or a campus is being relocated most healthcare leaders aren't going to take us on a spatial voyage; rather, they take us on a temporal one, into an uncertain and often unknown land: the future. The success of leaders in healthcare and also that of their followers will depend on how well they can read the horizon, anticipate the future of medicine, and make decisions that succeed in taking their groups and institutions into that future.

## CHALLENGES TO HEALTHCARE LEADERSHIP AND LEADERS

Great leadership has never been more important or more critical to the mission of healthcare. I had considered having a separate chapter or even section of the book to discuss the challenging times that we are living in.

Leadership Lessons for Health Care Providers. http://dx.doi.org/10.1016/B978-0-12-801866-8.00001-9

However, that topic is so big, so polemical, and so likely to change rapidly that I thought that a separate chapter or chapters would have distracted from our focus on our core mission in this volume. I decided instead to use this space to keep the focus on leadership, so the subsequent chapters will contain material about how healthcare leaders need to rise to these challenges. Today, healthcare faces severe threats and challenges on many fronts. In particular, declining reimbursement and rivalry with both traditional and nontraditional competitors in healthcare are eroding the political and economic fortunes of our fields. As this book goes to press, health care competition from nonhumans, from machines that can learn is evolving from science fiction to science fact. I interviewed many healthcare professionals for this book. As I talked with a wide spectrum of practitioners from cardiologists to nurses to psychologists and nurses there were several common themes. First and foremost was one of rapid change and even disruption of traditional practice in their fields. The second was that the future is far more uncertain than it had ever been in their careers, and a third was that the risks for us in healthcare practice have never been higher.

Many of the challenges start with the fact that healthcare is different than most other endeavors. To start with, the stakes are higher—people's lives, their bodies, and their emotional well being are all at stake. I have worked with successful leaders in a variety of fields outside of healthcare. While what they do is important, the risks of a mistake in selling clothes usually come down just to money—poor sales, failed marketing, etc. The mistakes in healthcare can be far more serious and far more damaging and have dimensions that are absent from some other types of leadership—the consequences are severe: pain, loss of health, and even loss of life itself are at risk. It is important to remember that the problems for healthcare leaders may also include both those of commission—a serious error—and those of omission—the services we can't provide to people because of waste, inefficiency, poor performance, etc.

## CHANGING HEALTHCARE

While change is difficult for many sectors of our society, it can be more difficult for healthcare leaders. When we consider change in healthcare, we are constrained on many sides by the degree to which healthcare is highly regulated. It isn't easy to get a new product or service approved quickly. A second challenge is that healthcare is often fragmented rather than integrated. While that type of environment creates some opportunities for change, it not only limits others but also limits the positive impact of change. For example, an improvement in care in the cardiac intensive care unit is an improvement, but if it is not combined with improvements that enhance care for patients elsewhere in the hospital and/or in outpatient experience, then the overall impact will be small. This will be just an isolated element with little impact on the patient and the larger society. Another challenge to change is that of costs. The pressures to reduce those costs have been discussed for decades, but are now coming to a head both on the private and public sides. The appetite in the public and private sectors to pay more for healthcare is very limited. The detailed discussion of medical costs and their impact on healthcare and society are beyond the scope of this book, but a few points should be made as they are directly germane to medical leadership.

## HEALTHCARE COSTS AND CHANGE

The costs of medicine are a function of many variables including those that are both intrinsic and extrinsic to the current medical system as we know it. Hospitals may be very good at taking care of gunshot victims. They may have good leaders who can effectively and efficiently mend bodies that are wounded by ballistic injuries. Effective leadership may keep the intrinsic costs under control. However, the total cost of that type of healthcare will still likely depend more on the level of gun violence in the hospital's referral area, which is an extrinsic cost to the hospital than it does on the intrinsic factors noted previously. A high level of gun violence leads to higher total costs to the system. Even an intrinsically efficient hospital would appear expensive if the extrinsic costs (ie., number of severely injured gunshot patients arriving each day) were high. This notion relates to many other aspects of extrinsic health costs, such as levels of cigarette smoking, obesity, recreational drug use, seatbelts, bike helmets, etc. As cost pressures increase and societal limits on spending are imposed, medical leaders will need to pay much greater attention to cost, quality, effectiveness, and related factors as they make decisions about how resources are used in medical practice.

The current challenges for leaders in healthcare however are about much more than cost. The structure of healthcare in the US is also being challenged. As this book goes to press there are pressures coming from several conflicting directions to change the current practice of medicine. One is a greater role of the Federal government in healthcare. While the states have historically had a lead role in regulating most aspects of medical practice in the United States, in recent decades the national government has had growing presence and influence through the expansion of Medicare, Medicaid, and the Veteran's Administration system with no sign that that those pressures will abate in the near future. Furthermore, Federalization of healthcare in this manner took a major step forward with the passage of the ACA in 2010.

The focus on changes in the public sector has led some leaders to miss the changes on the private side of the US healthcare sector. Change has also come from that side, as corporate involvement in healthcare has expanded in recent years with national companies moving into many kinds of medical practice. Simultaneously (and not coincidentally), many mid and late career physicians are giving up private practice for hospital employment. Meanwhile, many of the freshly minted physicians in the US are now going directly to employed positions in much greater numbers than in years past. Independent private practice is becoming a less available and perhaps for some a less desirable or realistic choice. This is creating a shift of both power and focus to the hospital rather than the physician practice or other entities as the core industrial unit of US healthcare. The implications of this transition for healthcare leadership are critical. If this trend continues it will affect who will be the leaders—will health care practitioners be led by their own or by nonphysicians. Furthermore it will also change the ways that they will lead and be led.

## HOW TO GET STARTED

So if I haven't scared you away from leadership in the first chapter, the next step is how you should get started in leadership. Before you do that, let's look at the interesting question of whether leadership is your work or someone else's. This is not a stupid question—in fact it is one that I hear being debated at medical meetings, business meetings, as well as in the hallways of hospitals. It has at least two elements: (1) should healthcare professionals lead in healthcare and (2) what should the structure of a healthcare organization look like, for example, how many leaders and what kind of leaders will it take for the institution to succeed. To answer the second one first, a recurring theme in this book will be that leadership means more than just the work of the top leader in a healthcare organization. It is not only a job for an executive at the top of a division or whole institution, but also the responsibility (and an opportunity) for many additional people, especially those of us who serve at the leading edge of the medical arts. In the broader sense, it is a set of tasks that is the responsibility of many of us who are healthcare professionals: physicians, nurses, dentists, technologists, pharmacists, therapists, administrators, and the many others who make the complex system of health run. That is also my answer to the first debate, you as a healthcare expert should be the kind of person who leads other healthcare experts. This is a polemical topic, but you can learn to be a leader, while many non-healthcare people who understand leadership could never learn to do your job. They can't really understand what it means to be a family physician, a nurse, or neurosurgeon or understand what really makes you a good dentist or psychiatrist.

I hope that inspires you to continue, but understand that you have some work to do. While you are probably an expert in your field, just being good at what we do in our area of expertise doesn't guarantee that we will be good leaders in healthcare enterprises. That experience, no matter how detailed or how many years you have been doing it, is by itself probably not enough for you to step directly into a high impact leadership role. Good leadership takes additional skills, extra work, and for many of us some extra training and education. Once you have made the effort to gain those newfound abilities, you will be in a position to make a real difference for yourself, for your organization, and for your career. Without sounding too prejudiced and at the risk of being a bit repetitious, you as a top tier health practitioner have insights into medical care and into the needs of patients that a top business school graduate is unlikely to ever acquire. The lessons in this book are designed to both teach these points and to inspire you to pursue a career that includes leadership.

At this point you may be asking what is leadership and what do leaders do? Don't worry, we will cover these topics and more in subsequent chapters. To get started, at the core, leadership is about helping to get a group of individuals to perform well in their mission as they move into the future. It isn't just about how smart you are (but smart is certainly good!). It isn't just about how good your medical and nursing and dental skills are (although good is important also). It isn't about how charismatic you are (but personability and charisma often help and it is safe to acknowledge that their lack can be problematic). It is about how well you can bring out the best in your group, whether that is a handful of people in a small practice or at the other end of the spectrum a large national medical organization with tens of thousands of employees. This book is about a journey, about both the decision to take it and the tools that you need to do it successfully.

Practical points. Each chapter will close with a series of key takeaway points. These will summarize the key points covered in the chapter and will focus on actionable points as well as those you should ponder prior to moving on to the next chapter.

## KEY POINTS

1. Being a leader is more than a title or a job, it is an activity.
2. Leadership is not about an individual, it is about rallying a group and bringing out the best in them.
3. Leaders take their groups on a journey. For us in healthcare, this is usually not a journey through space, rather it is through time, into the future.
4. Within the memory of those of us who currently work in healthcare, there has never been a more challenging time to work in US medicine.

*Image credit: A B-2 Spirit flies to the North Pole Oct. 27, 2011. U.S. Air Force photo/Bobbi Zapka*

# 2

# Profiles in Leadership: What Does it Mean to Be a Great Leader

*"Whatever can be done, will be done.*
*If not by incumbents, it will be done by emerging players.*
*If not in a regulated industry, it will be done in a new industry born without*
*regulation. Technological change and its effects are inevitable.*
*Stopping them is not an option."*
**—Andy Grove, business leader and former CEO of Intel Corporation,**
**1936-2016**

## DOES LEADERSHIP MATTER TO HEALTHCARE PROFESSIONALS?

Let's start this chapter with a set of important questions. First, do medical professionals need leadership? Don't nurses, doctors, and other healthcare workers know their jobs? They are some of the most highly trained (and tested and retested and certified and recertified, etc.) people in the US labor force. Do they really need leaders in their work sites? Well, the answer to this (for good and for bad) seems to be a resounding yes. Furthermore, it raises the very interesting questions of why and if so, who. As anyone who works in healthcare knows, we are beset with many pressures. These are related to a host of factors including the changing demographics of the society, the fiscal limits of societal spending on healthcare, and the rapid changes in healthcare delivery in both the public and private sectors.

Part of the need for leadership in the field is driven by the rapidity of that change. It is hard to find a dentist, a nurse, or a physician in the United States whose practice today is like that of a person in a similar role 25–30 years ago. The innovations are much more than merely that of our

Leadership Lessons for Health Care Providers. http://dx.doi.org/10.1016/B978-0-12-801866-8.00002-0

technological progress that the opening quote addresses. Those changes also encompass changes in how we pay for care, the role of consumerism in healthcare, and the rise of information sharing media, particularly the internet, etc. While predicting the future can be pretty difficult and unrewarding, it is probably a very safe prediction to say that the roles of those same folks 25–30 years in the future from today will at best only remotely resemble those of us in the present day. The drivers of change in the 21st century are legion and I suspect that the coming decades will be even more interesting than the two or three we have just lived through. The transformation that you will experience in the coming years will encompass a wide range of factors including economic, demographic, sociologic, and political in addition to the realm of technologic advancement. In the future, moreover, we will also have people working in healthcare who will have roles and jobs that don't even exist today. If you are sceptical about that sentence, think back 20 or 30 years and then look at the office in your hospital that manages data or the person or team that creates and manages your websites. Their jobs didn't exist back in the day. As the opening quote suggests, that process of innovation and change isn't over and probably won't ever be over for us in healthcare. One of the roles of a leader is to help a group to anticipate, to manage, as well as to cope with change and its impacts.

A second argument that medical people need leadership in order to succeed is the increase in managerial complexity of healthcare that has occurred as financial and institutional pressures have grown over the last several decades. Talking to people who worked in healthcare in the middle of the 20th century in healthcare is fascinating. While every generation has had it's challenges, it is fair to say that things really were different then. The systems in and around healthcare have grown much more complicated over the past 50 or so years—it is neither unrealistic nor trite to say that we really do live in more challenging times today. By necessity, as our practices adapt to respond to these challenges, we will need leaders who can develop coherent strategies and tactics to thrive (or at least survive). Success for us will require more than just putting up with change, but instead it will require finding resilient ways of adapting and responding to rapidly moving changes in the landscape in healthcare. To make it more emphatic, success will really go to those who not only put up with change or respond to it, but to those who can capitalize upon change and ride those waves successfully.

A third point, to which we will return in a subsequent chapter, is that leadership has an almost magical element in the performance of a group or organization. Many times in the course of our lives we deal in trade offs—do we hire more people so that we have more time off, but take a reduction in our salary as a result or in our personal lives do we want a bigger house or would we rather live in a smaller home, but take better vacations. Leadership can be different—with the right leader or leaders we might be able to get more success with the same resources. For example, take two groups of talented people. These can be rival medical groups, competing sports teams, two groups trying to provide agricultural aid in an under-developed part of the world, or even two armies. What then determines who succeeds or who loses? The quick answers that you often get first to that question often focus on which group has more talent, greater size, superior technology, better training, more experience, etc. Those are important factors, but when present they are often inadequate by themselves to predict success or failure. While we must also acknowledge: (1) that those core factors are important and (2) that there is always an element of luck and chance in our lives, the difference between winning or being mediocre or being a loser, is often that of organization and leadership. This is particularly important when those other factors that we started with are reasonably equivalent or closely balanced. Everyone has seen a group of five talented individuals lose a basketball game to five equally talented (or to make the case stronger, less talented individuals) who are better coached and managed. That is the secret ingredient that is (almost) magic in leadership and in disparate impact on predicting success and failure. On the positive side, it is about bringing out the best in a group. When it is done well it means that we can do better together. We can beat predictions based on other factors and succeed where others will fail.

## WHO SHOULD LEAD IN HEALTHCARE?

If we accept that healthcare needs leadership, it next follows that we need to figure out who should be a leader of healthcare professionals. Should it be one of our own, a woman or man like us who has walked the walk and spent time doing what we do, or will anyone with an MBA, a good suit, and a few years of business experience be able to do the job? Looking around the country at the variety of leadership structures, at first glance there is not an obvious answer to this question. I have lost count of the number of times that groups of medical professionals have asked me if I know a good student in one of my MBA programs who would be interested in being hired to lead their healthcare practice. Take a moment to note the terminology in the prior sentence—not to manage the office, not to run the financial side of the practice, both sensible and intelligent notions but rather to *lead* the practice. Operational expertise isn't the same as leadership. These are highly trained, well regarded, usually very good medical professionals, some of whom have made the lists of best doctors in their city. And yet they see themselves as too busy, too inadequate, or perhaps not enough of something else to be able to lead themselves and are willing to hire a stranger from outside of medicine to do this for them. Usually my advice begins with recommending that they rethink this idea rather than recommending an individual to do the job.

At the other extreme, there are some types of groups that are very un-likely to follow a leader who is not one of them. One of my uncles is a dec-orated fighter pilot and I have also had several students who flew combat missions for the US Air Force and Navy. These contacts have given me the opportunity and the honor to talk to them about their work, their training, and their culture. They would not be very likely to be led (at least effec-tively) by someone who was not a brother or sister pilot—someone who understood the pressures and perils that they face in their training and their missions. They almost certainly would not want to follow a 27-year-old MBA who had previously worked in the retail clothing sector. No matter how good they are at selling T-shirts, it probably won't transfer well to leading warriors. On the serious side, a leader (at least one with a chance of succeeding) needs to have a deep understanding of the issues that the members of the group face.

We (those of us in healthcare) are in the right position, in the right place, with the right training to see what needs to be done to make healthcare work well and to continue to make it work better. Someone who is work-ing with a difficult patient with a serious medical problem at 3:00 am has insights from being at the leading edge of care that a less involved per-son with a desk job from 8:00 am to 5:00 pm won't have and won't be able to completely understand. If your leader doesn't understand what is it like to nurse a sick child back to health or to treat an acute stroke or hold a beating heart in your hand, then they will have diminished or even absent effectiveness in trying to lead someone who does. Going back to our military analogy, someone who knows what it is like to fly upside down dodging enemy missiles is the kind of person who elite fighter pilots might be willing to follow. The person who had previously been selling T-shirts—not so much...

## KEY POINTS

1. The need for leadership in healthcare has never been greater.
2. Good leadership is not a commodity. Medicine is different than other sectors and requires unique qualities in it's leadership.
3. Healthcare professionals need leaders who have a deep understanding of the sector and are often best led by their own kind.

*Image credit: Theodore Roosevelt by John Singer Sargent, 1903*

# 3

# Deciding to Lead: When and Why to Begin to Take on Leadership Roles

*"Nothing is more difficult, and therefore more precious, than to be able to decide"*
**—Napoleon Bonaparte, French emperor, 1769-1721**

*"In any moment of decision the best thing you can do is the right thing, the next best thing is the wrong thing, and the worst thing you can do is nothing"*
**—Theodore Roosevelt, 26th President of the United States, 1858-1991**

*"Do or do not. There is no try"*
**—Jedi Master Yoda, fictional character, Star Wars (Episode V)**

## INTRODUCTION

In this chapter, we will explore the meaning of leadership, analyze case studies of both successful and failed leaders, and extract important lessons that can be applied in healthcare. Where possible we will use business case studies and historical examples to drive home many of the key points pertaining to your career and group. When we think of leadership, it often invokes a mental image of a successful alpha individual in government, the military, business, or sports. In some sense at least, as we noted previously leadership (at least in a rudimentary form) should be distributed in our organizations and not left up to one person or small group of people.

As we have noted earlier, these are times of great change and challenge to the healthcare system. This chapter will focus on decisiveness and is apropos of the discussion we have had on challenge—the times

Leadership Lessons for Health Care Providers. http://dx.doi.org/10.1016/B978-0-12-801866-8.00003-2

we live in will not tolerate delay and indecisiveness. If it makes you feel better (or perhaps not) while the focus of the settings in this book is on the US medical field, these challenges are essentially universal in nations that are similar to the United States. The issues: those of demographics, costs, limited budgets, societal priorities, and technological change are widely distributed (see Brus-Ramer, et al., in press). While those challenges are almost universal among countries that achieve certain levels of development, the solutions do vary significantly by country. This signifies the role that leaders can take in understanding best practices for healthcare across national boundaries. Great leadership has never been more important or more critical to the mission of health and healing and this need is not unique to any one country. The future is far more uncertain and the risks for us in healthcare practice have never been higher.

In this chapter, we will examine one of the most important functions of a leader—making important decisions—decisiveness. Leaders don't have the luxury of unlimited time to make every decision. The ability to make decisions, particularly the hard ones is a crucial feature of great leadership. Leaders need to weigh the urgency of a decision against the quality of information they have on hand. While some decisions can and should be delayed (at least for the right reasons), many cannot be delayed without incurring costs and damages to the organization and leaders who choose to procrastinate need to understand that most of us rarely ever get perfect information. A good leader has to be able to weight those risks and then be able to time their decisions, understanding that most decisions are made with imperfect information.

Equally important are some closely related facets of successful leadership (1) taking personal responsibility for decisions and their consequences and (2) sticking with hard decisions even when they have disruptive and difficult ramifications. Regrettably, these aspects of leadership are not always well displayed by so-called leaders in our society. Healthcare is no exception and probably has more than its share of deficiencies in this regard. A leader who can't or won't do those things will not only fail, but he or she will likely bring down their organization if they are allowed to continue along those lines of failure. A big part of the job of leader is helping the group decide, especially when the decisions are hard.

The challenge for some leaders is not so much their personal courage, but the nature of their groups. In fact, some healthcare groups have been described by an esteemed leader in my field of radiology, Dr. Larry Muroff, as suffering from a "pathology of democracy" (Dr. Larry Muroff, personal communication). I have seen this first hand for myself over the past decade in my consulting practice. In a variety of consulting projects across the United States with physicians, their groups, and their institutions, I have repeatedly seen groups that are unable to reach a consensus and act. Dr. Muroff's comment is spot on for one of the ills that our profession creates for itself. This is not a slur on democracy per se, and certainly not by me. Writing from the perspective of having both relatives and friends who were forced to live on the wrong side of the Iron Curtain under communist regimes has made me a big fan of the liberty and participatory democracy we enjoy in the free nations.

This paradox is a tough one at the group level and occasionally at the societal level. As is often the case, Winston Churchill probably said it best: "Indeed, it has been said that democracy is the worst form of government except all those other forms that have been tried from time to time" (*Hansard*, November 11, 1947). That said, the challenge is not whether to have democracy in our group or institutional settings, but rather how to harness the knowledge and capabilities of a diverse group to make democracy work.

One of these weaknesses of democracy (with a small "d" as it is practiced in healthcare groups) is the tendency to try to muddle through while avoiding or delaying the big hard decisions. Decisions that are often put off are those that will have adverse effects on the group, alienate factions within a group or institution, take large risks, require major investments, or involve substantial and rapid change, etc. Even when they face decisions and acknowledge the need, groups seem to sometime take forever to reach a consensus on how to handle a tough situation. Factions within a group or an institution may delay or prevent a decision from being made even when the issue at hand is vital to the well being of the partnership. Even when a decision appears to be made, it doesn't mean that the process is over. It can still take some healthcare groups an inordinate amount of time to implement strategic decisions and plans compared to organizations in many other sectors.

## MAKING AND STANDING BY TOUGH DECISIONS: A BUSINESS CASE STUDY

Business case studies and other examples from outside healthcare can drive home critical issues in leadership. One very useful example comes from a book that is one of the modern classics of management: *Good to Great*, by Jim Collins (2001). This book is particularly apropos for a discussion of leadership in that the author uses a scientific approach to investigating business and management outcomes. In this book, he and his team use companies with matched controls to ask questions about why companies succeed (or fail) when faced with challenges. Using metrics of success that are readily quantifiable (stock market performance over similar periods), they explore facets of management behavior that distinguish winners from losers.

In this chapter, we will deliberately go far afield from the medical world to make several key points about leading and decision making. In fact, we will go into the realm of consumer paper, the exciting world of products, such as disposable diapers and Kleenex. In the late 1960s the American consumer giant, Proctor and Gamble (P & G), entered this business sector, threatening the then existing leaders. The following case study is referenced from material in Chapter 2 in *Good to Great:*

In 1971, Darwin E. Smith took over as the CEO of Kimberly-Clark. A variety of factors and events had caused the stock to fall behind the market by 36% over the previous two decades. Early in his tenure, he concluded that the traditional core business of coated paper was a dead end and that there was a significant opportunity in consumer paper products. This required a radical redirection of the company including selling off their paper mills including their signature facility in Kimberly, Wisconsin. Beyond the extreme changes that this imposed upon his own organization, it also forced him into direct competition with P & G. It is not a stretch to say that this is analogous to giving up your current career in healthcare in order to start a software company to give Microsoft a run for its money in its core business. P & G is known for being a very well run, a very strong competitor that dominates many of its sectors. A decision to go head to head with P & G is not one that a serious leader would take lightly.

This was a decision that was opposed both internally and externally. It would have been easy for a lesser leader to put it off or dither away the opportunity in the face of so much antagonism. The business press was derogatory and Wall Street analysts punished the decision by downgrading the stock. At that point, it might have been tempting to slow down, do a little bit of one or the other or even go backward, but Mr. Smith kept going forward.

In his book, Jim Collins uses a good analogy here to the story (possibly apocryphal) of the Spanish conquistador Cortez destroying his ships upon arrival in Mexico. Whatever else ensued, for that army there would be no going back. By destroying the option of backing down, the group's commitment to the future of the decision was enhanced. Some decisions cannot be fudged. Sometimes you can't just muddle through—you have to make the decision, pick a path, and then forge ahead.

This case demonstrates the challenges that make a leader's job difficult. First, the decision involved a break with a proud tradition—never an easy decision in an institution or group with a strong, successful history. If you are working in medicine, you get this—we have a very proud tradition in this society. Without a doubt, there were many at the company who could not fathom why such radical changes were necessary and why the comfortable status quo could not be maintained. They undoubtedly hoped that the future would be kind to them and that at most only small, easy changes would be necessary. Resistance to change within an organization and specifically to your leadership goes with the territory when you decide to lead. Not everyone will love you and they certainly will not always agree with you or support you.

Second, it involved substantial and very serious risk. Taking on a world-class competitor like P & G would give rational business leaders serious pause. It would have been tempting for him to find a safer course during his tenure as leader of the company. These types of hard decisions, however, are exactly the job description of the CEO. They are supposed to identify the big important issues. That should be what they are getting paid for and when history is eventually written, it is an important aspect of how they will be judged.

Third, it triggered a significant backlash in public opinion. It is much harder to move forward in the face of substantial opposition particularly in the public eye. For you as the leader, it certainly might raise doubts about your decisions, if sophisticated experts are putting their own reputations on the line by disagreeing with you in the media. Also, at a practical level it makes it much harder to mobilize the troops if they get up in the morning and open up a business newspaper that questions their own leader's direction.

Ultimately, P & G smashed all the competition except for Kimberly-Clark. In fact, Kimberly-Clark actually beat P & G in six out of eight product categories. Its products, such as Huggies and Kleenex have become household names. In the case study in *Good to Great*, Kimberly-Clark is paired with Scott Paper. The latter company reacted to these same challenges from the marketplace in a very different fashion from Kimberley-Clark and did comparatively poorly. Not only did Kimberly-Clark beat out its competition, it ended up buying rival Scott Paper. Finally, in the ultimate hard edged, black and white quantitative measurement of relative American business success, Kimberly-Clark beat the general stock market indices by over four times during the 20-year study period.

This is a lesson in the hard decisions. Unfortunately for us in healthcare, we will have our share of difficult decisions to make in the coming years. How we choose and how we carry out those decisions will define our leadership and determine our success.

## KEY POINTS

If healthcare groups and institutions are to avoid the "pathology of democracy" described earlier and act more like the winner than the loser in the business case, several things must occur:

1. Leaders have to be invested with authority. Groups that choose a leader, but then don't give them the authority to lead and/or undermine their ability to lead will probably not do well in facing today's challenges.
2. Leaders need to tackle the hard choices. More than in any other decade or generation in recent history, we will need to make difficult choices about our future. Avoiding those choices will only make them harder and our position weaker.
3. Once a decision is made (provided you made it for the right reasons), you should be willing to stick by it. Now, I am not saying that decisions should always be fixed eternally in stone. In a future column we will discuss the right times and ways to reassess decisions and strategic plans and make course corrections if necessary. However, unless the world changes in the interim or new data arrive, be willing to stand your ground without wavering. Tough decisions require an element of courage.
4. Make decisions and stand by them for the sake of the greater good of your group and its future. If you want to win popularity contests, go back to high school or try out for a reality television show. In the short term at least, making hard decisions will almost always engender dissent and perhaps opposition. In the long run, if you are right you will be remembered as a visionary.

*Image credit: President Franklin D. Roosevelt delivering Fireside Chat #6*

# Your First 100 Days: Facing the Challenge of Becoming a New Leader

*"Real power can't be given. It must be taken"*
—*From "The Godfather - Part III", 1990 movie*

## INTRODUCTION

One of the greatest challenges in leadership occurs at the very beginning—when you take over as a new leader. Whether expected or unexpected, there are few times during your tenure as a leader when you will have so much opportunity to get it right (or wrong). Most private (and some academic) healthcare practices promote from within and this chapter will focus on that situation. However, much of this advice will also serve you well if you come in from outside instead.

The aforementioned movie quote is to make the point that you don't just move into a position when you become a leader. You also need to make it your own. Power isn't just given to you, you must make your mark and take control. In that sense, setting the right tone from the beginning is crucial to your success. Leadership, at least the good kind, is a hefty responsibility. There is a unique intensity to your job. You are a very special face and voice of your organization. You will receive a disproportionate share of the praise and blame for the path the practice takes during your tenure. There is no single recipe for success here or elsewhere. However, there are several pieces of advice regarding common mistakes of omission and commission that should be taken to heart in order to succeed in your new position.

Leadership Lessons for Health Care Providers. http://dx.doi.org/10.1016/B978-0-12-801866-8.00004-4

# YOUR FIRST 100 DAYS: HIT THE GROUND RUNNING HARD... VERY HARD

The phrase "the 100 days" probably originated with Napoleon. However, for him it was an end to leadership, not a beginning; his last grasp at power after his abdication and initial exile to Elba but before his final defeat at Waterloo and his ultimate banishment to Saint Helena. In more recent usage in US, it is often reworded as the "first 100 days" and that term is usually attributed to the beginning of President Franklin Delano Roosevelt's first term in 1933. Few other presidents have grappled with as great a challenge as he did at the beginning of his first term. He entered into his role of leadership while facing the darkest period to date in US economic history. While economists continue to this day to examine and analyze (and argue over) the efficacy of his efforts, there is no doubt that he responded to the crisis with a remarkably active agenda. His White House pushed 15 major pieces of legislation through Congress in its first 100 days, creating much of what has become known as the New Deal. In the process, this greatly expanded the role of the Federal government including a large number of new governmental agencies (White, 2006).

Ever since, US presidential administrations usually begin with an analogous campaign to get as many key pieces of legislation or other projects accomplished early. This signals that a new crew is in charge and that the new leader is capable of getting things done. The rest of us should also try to implement our agendas quickly, and the 100 day target is an excellent personal goal for implementing the changeover to your leadership from the previous administration. Here is how you can get started.

## Change in a Position Requires Both Internal and External Changes

The first step in taking a leadership position is to change your mental framework. You have to start acting like a leader. The cliché—"its lonely at the top" may not always be true, but a surer truism is that it will be different for you and for those around you. You need to be ready to signal that you are in charge. If you don't act the part, it is unlikely that you will be accepted as a leader. It is worth repeating here, that you need to "take" power at the beginning. If you delay doing this, you may have a great deal of trouble later. Leaders sometimes have a surprisingly short period to make it clear that the transition has occurred. You need to make an impact, make it clear that there is a new person in charge.

Now that you are the leader, you will need to adapt and you will also need to help those around you adapt to the change in your relationship. Healthcare practice leaders are often chosen internally. As you settle into your new position remember that other folks probably wanted the job and you were promoted past them. The envy that goes with this may harm your friendship unless you set an appropriate tone in the group. The challenge is there whether you came from inside or from without, but the personal dynamics will depend upon your history with the group.

## Gather as Much Information as You Can

This is the best time to ask stupid questions. This is your honeymoon period so make the most of it. In our teaching practices, we expect and tolerate (at least most of us) stupid questions from the trainees. We all become tougher as people move along in their training, so use the unique opportunity you have at the beginning to cover the basics. A related issue is that this is the best time to turn over the rocks and see what is lurking underneath, making sure that you peek into all the dark corners of your practice. You will look very foolish if you wait until the second year of your tenure to ask an important question, such as why one of your hospital contracts is so badly designed or why there are serious flaws in how you are doing your service and quality programs.

This is a crucial time to listen more than you talk. This is a time to collect information, not show off how much you know. You should be seeking information from both inside and outside of your organization. You should try to get to as many national meetings in healthcare as you can to get a broad perspective on what is going in our very complicated profession. It is an opportunity to talk to your peers and see how they are handling the types of challenges that are now landing on your desk. Here is a short list of the folks that you should get to and interview (if possible):

1. **The person you are replacing.** Sometimes this is impossible. They may have left under a cloud. There may be bad feelings or some form of confidentiality agreement that precludes them from talking with you. However, if you can get to them and have a conversation, this is one of the ways that you can jump start your insertion into the role. Try to understand their leadership style, their relationships, where they succeeded, where they fell short, and don't forget what is sometimes the most important question—why did they leave?
2. Savvy business students will tell you that the latter question should be extended to other folks who looked at the job and passed. If you were internally promoted in a five person dental group this won't be a very illuminating answer, but it can be quite important in many other circumstances. If other very smart, very capable candidates from out of town or out of state looked at your hospital and decided not to take the job, or worse ran away from it, you might want to understand

what made them uninterested or in the worse case frightened by the job. Understanding their reasons for passing on the job may give you a lot of insight into the challenges that you will need to overcome to succeed in your new position.

3. Meet with all your key stakeholder groups. Don't limit this just to a hospital administration. Make sure that you go further and set up meetings with your patients to discuss what they like and dislike about your current practice. Get out and talk to your physicians and other clinical colleagues. If you can, visit their offices and meet everyone including the nurses, nurse practioners, physician assistants, and all the other groups who may also be your customers (Lexa, 2006).

4. Meet with the top-level folks within your organization as soon as you know that you will be taking over. Ask them the key questions enumerated in the next section.

5. Use "skip level" meetings to go past your peer group and make sure that get to everyone in your organization. These are meetings where you meet with people at least two layers below you in the organization. The key element is to meet with them *without* the intervening folks present. These "skip" meetings help you to reach out to the members of the group that may not normally have direct access to the leader. Try to get the unvarnished truth about how things work. You often do better when you listen to people who are very different than you and the other professionals like you. For example, if you are a clinician–leader, make sure that you sit down with groups, such as the technical staff directly and listen to them. Reach out to the groups that you depend on, but probably don't talk to enough. Depending upon the size and structure of your group, you may need to meet with the nonpartnership/part time employees separately. These meetings will give you a much broader perspective on your situation. That view will be essential to you in the coming days in order to be able to craft winning strategies and tactics for the practice.

6. Build a network of mentors and friends (outside the practice) so that you can have a sounding board. These are the people who can hear you out and give you advice that is free of the taint of internal agendas and politics within the walls of your institution. Everyone needs a friend (or better friends) who they can call for a second opinion on leadership issues.

## The Right Questions to Ask Internally

Often I am asked: what should I be doing in these meetings in my first 100 days? Here are some questions that you should be using internally. If used skillfully, they help you get the information you need while sending a strong message to your team that you will be a capable leader in tough times (adapted from Neff and Citrin, 2005):

1. What are the top three things that we need to preserve and protect our practice at Metropolis Health care?
2. What are the top three things that need to be changed here?
3. What are you concerned that I will do during my time as a leader?
4. What are you concerned that I will not do during my time here?

## Have an Agenda and Implement it Aggressively

Transitions come in several forms. You may have been waiting in the wings for years thinking about this day, while at the other extreme, your current leader may have stepped down suddenly for personal or health reasons and you are thrust on the stage. In any case, you need to come on board with a plan as quickly as possible and show everyone who is watching that you are capable of leading and implementing. This doesn't necessarily mean that you should arrive on day one with a 100 page business plan for the practice. However, you should have a plan to create the plan in the first 3 months of your tenure. Much of that plan will be built out of the information gathering described previously. Here are some suggestions for this phase of your tenure.

## Keep Asking Yourself: What Is My Agenda?

In the corporate world there is often an interval called the "countdown period" between announcing a new leader and his or her starting the new position. If that happens to you, the scrutiny actually will begin the moment that you are publically identified as the heir apparent and that should be when you make your agenda so that you can then start in high gear (Neff and Citrin, 2005). If you are fortunate to have a countdown period, make the most of it and if possible adjust the length of it so that it can work to your advantage. You should have an agenda that you can begin to implement it on or perhaps even to some extent before you officially start. As you go forward, you should keep asking yourself a few questions: "What is my agenda?", "Is it still the right agenda?", and "Do my actions align with my agenda for this position?"

## Set Appropriate Expectations

When you set expectations, you need to find a "Goldilocks" solution: one that takes a middle path that is just right. Leaders can get off on the wrong foot if they don't succeed and instead veer off in one of two directions, that is, by either promising too little or too much. In the former, those who come in without setting a strong tone of leadership are often perceived as weak, not likely to stay around for very long, or just clueless or perhaps a combination of all three.

However, at the other extreme, big promises early in your tenure will be remembered. If you promise to expand the hospital, or to get a better contract for your fellow nurses or bring in a big piece of state of the art technology, you have an obligation and your colleagues will not forget it. If you made these promises because you hadn't gotten your information right, you will be seen at best as foolish and at worst as a shallow or stupid leader. If you break promises for other reasons, you will be seen as untrustworthy or perhaps worse and your effectiveness within the organization will be significantly limited.

A good strategy in the early phase of your leadership career is to balance big long-term goals that can galvanize a group and motivate them with some smaller, short term wins that you can accomplish relatively early in your tenure that will build morale and cement your image as a successful leader.

## Build Your Team

One of the most commonly cited success factors in the business literature is getting the right people on board. A leader needs a supportive, capable team. Getting them and building them into a cohesive team is a critical, if not an existential task for a healthcare leader. Sometimes though this can be hard. In the medical arenas, we often inherit teams and moving or firing the wrong people is not as easy as in other work setting. If you can't simply get rid of the people you don't walk and hire the ones that you do think belong on the team, sometimes we can build or rebuild a team to get it right (Watkins, 2003). In the whatever circumstances you find yourself in, to the extent you can, follow the mantra of Jim Collins in *Good to Great*: "first who, then what" (Collins, 2001).

Unfortunately (or fortunately depending upon your perspective), many healthcare leaders have little ability to fire physician partners (absent extraordinary circumstances). Nevertheless, you do have the ability to influence hiring and promotion. Moreover, all leaders need to develop a core group that they can trust. The term "kitchen cabinet" dates back to President Andrew Jackson. This phrase refers to an informal group of trusted advisors that leaders bring together to help them work with their real Cabinet secretaries (for further details about the term "kitchen cabinet", see http://en.wikipedia.org/wiki/Kitchen_Cabinet). This is an important concept. In addition to your actual team of coworkers, it is helpful to have a "virtual" team of advisors, mentors, and other friends to help you. You need to develop a group with a "circle of trust" to make things happen for you in the larger organization.

## Reach Out

In the 21st century in the US, most healthcare leaders do not act like dictators, but rather function more like prime ministers. By that I mean that they can't dictate policy and expect blind obedience, but instead need to build both a constituency within the organization as well as a relative consensus in order to be able to govern effectively. Unless you are in a small intimate group, this is more than the circle of trusted advisors described previously. You need to listen to the group members, sound them out, try to understand their capabilities, limitations, and goals. Always remember that politics is the art of the possible and that your group's members will have a very strong influence on what will be possible to accomplish in your tenure.

Great leadership is not just support from a majority of your partners. When we say to reach out you need to go further than your group or department. The most successful healthcare leaders I have met understand that they must also build relationships with a wider network of other constituencies. These include all the entities you serve directly or indirectly: hospitals, academic institutions, payers, patient groups, and the government. You should plan (or develop a plan) for reaching these groups during the first phase of your tenure.

## Where Do You Go From Here?

In the crush of getting settled in remember that there will be another 100 days (hopefully) so you must be prepared to execute and move forward beyond the initial period. In conclusion, here are the points that you can use to keep it on track as you come to the end of the beginning:

1. A good target is the following: Look hard at your value as a leader and then make it your goal to reach a "break even" point in your contribution as a leader where you have increased the value of your organization beyond the cost of your time and effort? This will happen faster if you make a strong commitment.
2. Write down your goals. Make them specific, including times of completion.
3. Review the plan regularly. You won't accomplish it all in the first 100 days or even the first 1000, but you will accomplish much more and be better prepared for the unknown if you make this a serious, concrete commitment.

## KEY POINTS

1. Start hard and fast in your leadership role.
2. Have a plan for how to start.
3. Address the aforementioned steps—they will get you started and help you develop good leadership habits.
4. Great leadership in the first 100 days will lead to new challenges in the next hundred and beyond. This is what makes the journey fun and rewarding.

*Image credit: A full-scale model of a C-5 Galaxy cockpit.*
*U.S. Air Force photo/Senior Airman James Bolinger*

# 5

# The Unexpected Leader: Challenges of Having Leadership Thrust Upon You

*"Dans les champs de l'observation le hasard ne favorise que les esprits préparés"*
*(In the fields of observation chance favors only the prepared mind)*
**—Louis Pasteur, French scientist, 1822-1895**

## INTRODUCTION

Being suddenly thrust into an important leadership role without adequate preparation is frightening (at least for most sane people). It can make the 100 days that we discussed earlier feel like a vacation. In my consulting work with health professionals, though, I have helped several people deal with the situation of being the "unexpected leader." Some of them were totally surprised and some were totally unprepared and as you can imagine some struggled with both. A few had expected to take on a leadership role, but just not that year and in one case, not that decade. This situation can arise for a variety of reasons—the previous leader had been fired, had a health issue, had just been indicted (or worse convicted—yes, that was an interesting one...), or just got fed up and quit unexpectedly. Regardless of the reason for the sudden vacancy, for the new leader who has just had the role thrust onto his or her shoulders the problems are the same: how do I quickly get control of the situation and then start to become a capable leader?

One of leaders who I have worked with described it to me as feeling like they just answered the dreaded call on a transoceanic flight—"Is there anyone on board who can fly a plane?" The problem is that other than occasionally playing with a flight simulator on their home PC, they really don't have any experience with flying airplanes (and no one else

Leadership Lessons for Health Care Providers. http://dx.doi.org/10.1016/B978-0-12-801866-8.00005-6

answered the call). The combination of unexpected responsibility, little or no preparation, and a paucity of options makes for a personal crisis and a crisis for your group. In this chapter we will discuss how to reduce the risk from landing in this situation totally clueless (prevention and preparation) and what to do when it does happen despite your best efforts.

## PREPARATION

There is an old cliché in sports that applies well here. You shouldn't be on the sidelines unless you want to go into the game. If you aspire to be a leader, then don't treat it as something in the category of "things that I will do someday." In addition to the cliché that someday never comes, there are two important observations here. First, follow the admonition of Dr. Pasteur. Start preparing today if you want to be a leader. If you are prepared, you have a much greater chance of success. Life is full of times when chance, fate, karma, or God will present you with opportunities.

In this case, if you are hoping to be a leader, then do more than hope—start learning, try to get more responsibilities, and begin doing work in leadership long before the big day. That will put you in good stead whether your day comes on schedule or as a big surprise.

## PREVENTION BY PAYING ATTENTION

Pay close attention to your current leaders and the situation in your institution. As a sophisticated insider you do have some advantages that you can use. While it is rarely as obvious as a scene from a movie where people are burning and shredding all the office records or flying out of the US on a one way ticket to a country without an extradition treaty, you should be able to pick up on signals that bad things are happening before they are obvious to an outsider. Moreover, if you are being groomed as a future leader and your current leader trusts you, he or she may give you some warning that things are about to change and change fast. Pay attention to him or her. Many people are too proud to admit they are tired of leadership or are no longer up to the job. They may not tell you directly, but they may send subconscious signals that they are getting ready to bail out.

## PARACHUTING IN

So whether or not you have done your best to prepare for the big day and whether or not you have tried to anticipate changes in your situation, the big event occurs. Now, all of sudden in your institution (or elsewhere) you are an instant leader. We will now examine this tough, but not that rare situation in leadership. The strategies you need are a hybrid of those that we discuss in detail in the 100 days chapter with those discussed in the chapter on how to handle crisis leadership. You need to move fast, but not so fast that you create more problems and trouble for yourself and those you serve than you are successfully fixing.

## Step 1: Have a Meeting With the Person or Persons or Group That Has Asked You to Lead

Make sure that you take accurate notes and that you understand their expectations. Make sure that you slow down enough to ensure that you have the resources that you need to do the job and to do it well. Those of us in healthcare have been trained to be helpers. In healthcare, we are in the helping professions. We self select and are trained to help others. This means that our reflex in a tough situation is to try to help and we often say yes quickly when presented with problems. Yet we need to take stock to make sure that we have the people, equipment, and other assets we need to do the job that we are about to take on. We can't overpromise at this point, nor can we do it all ourselves. Make sure at the end of the meeting or meetings, that you verify the terms and expectations. Whether you send a letter or use an email, make sure that you confirm these issues with a message that says "based on our meeting today, I will do ..., I will receive the following resources..., etc." Speed, urgency, and the other factors in play here sometimes make us rush through the niceties, but make sure that you have a written record of at least the big, critical elements of what you promised and what was promised to you. That may turn out to be a very valuable document in a year or two.

## Step 2: If Possible, Meet With and Debrief the Person Who Has Just Left

While your situation won't be identical to theirs, anything that they can tell you is likely to be of interest and can help you make it through the first stage of your leadership role. Ask probing questions about who they could trust (and who they couldn't) in the organization. Insights that they can provide about how to get things done and what projects to take on now (as well as which ones to avoid) will help you to accelerate your effectiveness. In some corporate situations, this may be impossible due to confidentiality agreements. If you can speak to him or her, then the next best thing is to intensively find out what you can about them, perceptions about them, the politics of the position, etc.

## Step 3: As I Outlined in the Prior Chapter, Meet With the Key People at Every Level in Your Organization as Quickly as Possible

Spend more time listening than talking. Moreover, BE CAREFUL WHAT YOU PROMISE. Sorry for the all caps, but this is a mistake that many new leaders make, particularly those who are under stress. As much as you need to get allies and neutralize opponents ASAP, don't compromise your effectiveness and integrity by making promises that you won't be able to keep. Saying "I don't know" or "I just got here, so let me take a look at that and let you know" may feel like weasel words or sound indecisive they may be the best, most honest answers that you can give when you are swamped and still putting out fires and getting oriented.

## Step 4: Set Priorities for Both the First 100 Days, but Also for Your Leadership Tenure

It may sound extreme to say to begin with the end in mind when you are barely in your office, but the sooner you develop an outline of what you are going to try to do in the longer term, the more likely you plan for how to achieve your goals. This is a big challenge for the "unexpected" leader. Many of us in healthcare are well trained to react in a crisis. In fact, many of us are classified as "first responders," "first receivers," etc. We know how to react to a traumatized patient, a code blue call, or in my case circumstances like a potentially fatal contrast reaction. Our reflex when we are called unexpectedly to lead is to treat it like a crisis. There isn't anything wrong with this. In fact, if you have a smart, tested, structured approach to this (like you would for a nursing or surgical emergency) that is good and that is one of the things that this chapter is trying to impart. But the teaching for Step 4 here, is to remind you that you also need to start thinking beyond the crisis. If you stay on as the leader, then start working on the longer term issues as quickly as you can.

## Step 5: Build a Team of Capable People Who You Can Trust

One of the themes of this book is that while it may at times be lonely as a leader, the best leaders find ways to build robust networks and teams to help support the leader and her or his agenda. The network doesn't need to have all nurses or doctors or other folks like yourself, whatever your background. In fact, building a network of people from other levels and departments of the institution will give you more strength than just surrounding yourself with likeminded individuals. Even if you are more comfortable with fellow physicians, your short (and also longer term) success will likely depend on casting a wider net.

**TABLE 5.1** Impact Versus Time Matrix for Leadership Priorities

| Less important | Existential | |
|---|---|---|
| Opportunity to get a discount on a key piece of equipment | Major IT collapse Abusive or incompetent employee | Short time window |
| Redecorating the waiting room to make it more patient friendly | Need to hire a key employee by next year | Not time critical in short run |

## Step 6: Spend Time Prioritizing What Needs to Be Done

One way to respond to the overwhelming nature of this situation of unexpected leadership is to create a simple starting point to create a 2 × 2 matrix (Table 5.1). Separate things that are truly existential—I need to do this or my group (and/or I) will seriously suffer from the things that would be good to do but that won't have a critical impact on the survivability of the institution or department or you personally. Then further separate things that have a short time window—those that are urgent and need to be addressed (or dismissed) either now or in the very near future versus those which allow you more time to collect additional information and make a more leisurely decision. While procrastination is not usually a virtue, this is a situation where it can be justified. In a crash introduction to leadership it can be wise to delay some decisions at this point for two reasons. First, all of us have human limitations including the amounts of attention and stamina that we can bring to bear in our jobs. In a critical situation like this, you need to focus on the more important issues and will have to deliberately ignore others. Second, some decisions will be better made if you require additional information gathering and will improve your judgement.

In the matrix that you have created, things that go into the upper right box should be those at the top of your list of priorities. A key person who comes into your office on day one and threatens to quit and take other people with them unless you make good on promises that your predecessor made to her or him definitely belongs in that quadrant. So does someone who is incompetent at taking care of patients and/or who is abusive to other personnel. These are critically important things that need to be handled very quickly. At the bottom left are the things that many leaders (including the good ones) think about but may never get to. They may never have the time or the resources to do them and so these often get considered but never actually done. Neither time urgency nor a serious threat drives the leader to make a decision about these ones. When they get done, it is because they represent "easy" wins that require little financial or political capital.

For many leaders, the hard decisions involve weighing time versus importance in deciding whether to work on the top left or lower right quadrants. For you in the position of doing a highly accelerated start to your job, it is safe to say that you should make sure that you have either cleared out or at least develop strategies for handling the urgent/existential quadrant before spending much time elsewhere in the grid.

Notice that there is no cell for the unimportant things. One of the few advantages of leading in a crisis, or in the case of this chapter, beginning to lead in a crisis is that you simply won't have time to spend on the unimportant and/or stupid things that some leaders get bogged down within their jobs. Whether they are urgent or not, unimportant things are still unimportant. I have yet to meet a leader who feels that they have too much time. One of the lessons of the time starvation that you will feel if you are thrust into leadership is that you can safely ignore many things that might seem important if you had a lot of free time. Great leaders need to be able to focus on what matters most—first things first. Moreover, occasionally I have seen people use trivia to distract themselves from focusing on the big important issues. In my consulting work, when I see a leader in this situation focusing on something like the color of the carpet in the waiting room, it means that they are pathologically frightened of the important crises going on around them. Obsessing about trivia temporarily diverts attention to a safer, more comfortable place. The resulting procrastination and neglect just makes things worse over the long run. My job is to help them get over their fears and get them to reengage with big issues.

## Step 7: Set an Agenda for Your Goals

When people are setting priorities or doing time management sometime usually means "not now" which often results in never going to happen. Look at the matrix (or if you prefer a linear approach, then create a priority list—whatever works for you in setting your leadership agenda). Then get to work on a plan. Things are much more likely to go your way if you start to lay out the "when" of what you want to do. Since most significant projects occur as a series of steps or milestones, this will also help you with conceptualizing the "how" of your leadership work projects, that is, how you break a project down into manageable chunks. This is often the key for procrastinators and for those who are fearful. There shouldn't be shame in being afraid. At times that merely means that you are rational and paying attention. There are times in our lives when we should be afraid. The key is to use that fear to energize our efforts to deal with legitimate threats. Developing a plan to handle threats is the key to step #7.

## KEY POINTS

In this chapter we have focused on a situation that combines elements of handling a crisis with how to begin your tenure as leader. While it may never arise in your career, the insights here will help you with those that definitely will—all careers have a starting point and all leaders will face crises of one magnitude or another.

1. Start by defining your mandate and learning as much as you can from previous and current stakeholders.
2. Accelerate your integration into the leadership role, but don't be so hasty that you make foolish decisions and promises in your rush to make friends and allies.
3. Prioritize and categorize what needs to be done and when in your launch period.
4. Don't be afraid to ignore unimportant things if they get in the way of more critical things. Sometimes you will make mistakes in ignoring a small thing that turns out later to be important, but that is not an excuse for ignoring the burning problems in front of you.

*Image credit: Georges Clemenceau. From the George Grantham Bain collection at the Library of Congress.*

# 6

# Leading From Below

*"La guerre! C'est une chose trop grave pour la confier à des militaires"*
*(War is too important to be left to the generals)*
—*attributed to Georges Clemenceau, physician and twice Prime*
*Minister of France, 1841–1929*

To paraphrase what may have already been a paraphrase of one of Clemenceau's many colorful quotes, leadership is too important to be left to the leaders. In medicine, we are often accused of having too much democracy in our groups (Lexa, 2010a). With the distribution of power should come responsibility by a wider group for leadership. In some groups of knowledge workers, elements of leadership are distributed among many members of the group. All of us in healthcare should have opportunities to lead within our practices right now regardless of our job titles. Furthermore, most of us should be preparing now to take on more leadership activities as we move forward in our careers. Today, we will specifically address how we can and should lead even when we aren't the current Chair or the President or CEO.

Roger Fisher and Alan Sharp wrote an interesting book a while back on how to lead regardless of your nominal position in a group or institution (Fisher and Sharp, 1998). It nicely addresses this very tough situation that many of us in healthcare face—how do we start to lead when see opportunities, but we are not the leaders. In years past, the answer might have been to "manage up," that is, influence your leader to address the issues that you see. In this century, when we talk about distributed leadership and information flows in knowledge organizations, a different answer is to start leading at your level.

The book is entitled *Getting It Done: How to Lead When You're Not in Charge*. This is a nice book for those of us who are not the named leaders—at least not yet. As both professionals and "knowledge workers," healthcare workers are in particular need of this type of advice. We have enormous potential for leadership, yet too few of us seek out leadership roles. This is to both our personal detriment as well as to our organizations.

Leadership Lessons for Health Care Providers. http://dx.doi.org/10.1016/B978-0-12-801866-8.00006-8

41

For medicine to thrive in difficult times, more knowledgeable front line professionals need to participate in both formal and informal leadership.

In their book, Fisher and Sharp summarize the process of leadership as involving the following elements: purpose, thinking, learning, engagement, and feedback. This is an action oriented and project-based methodology for structuring your leadership activities. This can be applied whether you are at the top, the middle, or the bottom of an organization. In this column, there is only space to provide a limited treatment of their approach, but it is a good starting point for readers who want to do better on their next leadership challenge.

Fisher and Sharp start their analysis of the activity of leadership at the right place—the beginning. First have an aim—deciding the goals that you want to achieve. This is more than a vision statement. This is a forward-looking goal or a set of goals. It helps to make those goals as clear, detailed, and coherent as possible. For those of us leading from the middle or from below, a goal can be very simple and pragmatic—improving report turn-around time by X, raising patient satisfaction by Y, or decreasing unread studies from the weekend by Z, etc. Quantification is not only helpful, it is usually a requirement. Airy pronouncements about being the "greenest medical group in the tri state area" are fine, but are inadequate without specifics. When you specify the details, such as how much, where, and when then these goals move from the fantasy world of the mission statement into operational reality. When you lead from below, you need to set very specific goals. The better you are at bringing these goals into focus and finding concrete end points, the better you will be at leading a project in your institution. One point that is often left out, even though it seems obvious, is to have a deadline as part of your targeting. When will you have the new PACS (Picture Archiving and Communications System— the system that displays and controls the flow of images in the radiology system) fully operational? By when will you have no cases being left over from the weekend, etc.

Next you move on to the question of how you will do this. The authors call this phase—thinking. This is more than just speculating or doing a quick and dirty outline. This means rigorous disciplined approaches to figuring out how you will achieve your purpose. This is the "how will we do it". Aggressive goals, such as "we will halve our report turnaround time by the end of the summer" will likely require aggressive methods. It is both useless and frustrating to you and your organization to set big hairy audacious goals if you are clueless about how to achieve them. You need to think through both how you will do this and what the potential downsides are. Will there be moral hazards? that is, people working too fast, perhaps cutting corners, not playing well with others and/or other adverse behaviors and outcomes.

Learning is the next phase. As you implement your ideas, do you pay close attention? Do you catch both the expected and unexpected results of your project in time to manage them well or do you only see the key issues in retrospect. How well did your predictions work? Where did you do both better and worse than you expected? Do you (or perhaps your group) have a formalized way to learn from your experience. Are you looking continually at how you do things? Things that can help you here are to review early and often. One of the best ways to do this in a disciplined fashion is to have a mechanism for doing what the military calls an "after action" analysis. Once the project is completed, do a full review that addresses all of the aforementioned learning points.

For a project to work, you as the leader can't do everything. By definition, leadership involves a group interaction and effective leadership hinges on getting the group involved. In this arena, which the authors call engagement, you need to ask questions, such as: are tasks assigned? Do your key people all have tasks? Are they appropriate to the person? Your people should be pushed but not overwhelmed. Are the elements of work, the responsibility, and the potential rewards appropriately distributed?

Integrated into the above is another key element, that of feedback. As a group, do you have ways to give and receive feedback. Going to the next level, are there formal mechanisms for mentoring and coaching? How is advice given and taken? Does everyone get a say? Are there ways to reward/punish negative behaviors? Are you using smart mechanisms or dumb, that is, as we discussed previously are you implementing policies that invite moral hazards and adverse outcomes?

Leaders whether they are at the top, the middle, or the bottom of an organization need to develop effective techniques for leading. Even if you are not the person with the title in your organization you can lead at your level and make major contributions.

## KEY POINTS

1. Regardless of where they are in an organization professionals can and should find ways to lead. They can begin to lead regardless of their title.
2. Formal approaches to leadership activities can improve outcomes for leadership at all levels in an organization.
3. Most health professionals are in work settings where there are opportunities both formal and informal to begin to work on leadership projects.
4. To paraphrase, Georges Clemenceau, in the types of organizations most medical people practice within, leadership is simply too important to be left just to one person.

*Image credit: Portrait of President Harry S. Truman (ca. November 1945).*

# 7

# Qualities of Great Leadership

"Misleaders"
—*Peter F. Drucker, American author, 1909-2005*

"*Whoever is careless with the truth in small matters cannot be trusted with important matters.*"
—*Albert Einstein, theoretical physicist, 1879-1955*

"*It is amazing what you can accomplish if you do not care who gets the credit.*"
—*Harry S. Truman, American politician and 33rd President of the United States, 1884-1972*

## INTRODUCTION

A large part of an introduction to leadership in the early 21st century involves a component of myth busting. Leadership is commonly misunderstood within our society and probably even more so in some medical sectors. In this chapter, we will explore both what leadership is and what it isn't. This is essential for developing leadership skills both in ourselves and in the next generation. This analysis is also critical for understanding how and why we give power and authority to leaders as well as how we relate to other leaders.

The misconceptions about what constitutes good leadership have been amplified in recent years in our media obsessed society. The "celebrity CEO" has become a common and sometimes unfortunate element of the modern landscape in corporate America as well as in some other parts of the world. In an earlier chapter, we looked at a case study from "*Good to Great* (Collins, 2001) and saw his insights into why otherwise similar organizations can have very different performance and outcomes due to significant differences in their leadership.

In another portion of that work, the author discusses how often great business leaders seem to be almost exactly the opposite of the egomaniacal characters who often dominate the cable news financial channels. Rather,

Leadership Lessons for Health Care Providers. http://dx.doi.org/10.1016/B978-0-12-801866-8.00007-X

they are thoughtful, hard working folks who are much more concerned about the greater good of their people and their organization than their selfish needs. This is not unique to business and is certainly true in some other arenas as well. As someone once commented about American Presidents, we would usually be much better off with people of character in that role rather than people who are characters. This is just as true in most other serious organizations including our own medical organizations. Unless you work for the circus, you shouldn't be hiring clowns—especially for the top jobs. In this chapter, we will turn to another expert for a discussion on what it means to be a leader and what it takes to do it well.

## AN EXPERT'S VIEW ON LEADERSHIP

Peter Drucker is one of the world's most respected observers and writers on issues in business management. As he points out in "Leadership as Work" (Drucker, 2001, p. 268-271) leadership skills are often mistakenly confused with charisma. This error is dangerous for two reasons. First, as Mr. Drucker notes, some of the most horrifying leaders in world history have also been among the most charismatic. The 20th century's top three list of mass murderers—Stalin, Hitler, and Mao—were also in their own rather odd ways also charismatic men in their day. Even more strange is the continuing adulation that they receive even in death. Despite their hideous atrocities, each of them are still revered in some quarters to this day. All three of them created disasters and are certainly neither ethical role models nor models for emulating leadership for lasting success.

This is not to completely denigrate personal magnetism and charm. Certainly, these factors can be an enormous help for a leader, particularly one who faces significant challenges and obstacles. It would be hard or more likely even impossible to lead change in the world if you are terribly unlikeable, utterly withdrawn, and usually unpleasant. Personal charisma has been an aid and often a requirement for the success of some great leaders. Dr. Martin Luther King, Jr. and Mohandas Gandhi embodied many of the positive principles we are about to discuss, and they were also extraordinarily charismatic leaders as well as likeable, pleasant folks by many accounts.

The second reason for this discussion and from my perspective the more compelling point, is that this focus on the mystique of the "Great Man or Great Woman" and on their magical charisma obscures and often even precludes a serious examination of the real things that leaders need to do to succeed. Treating leadership as a strange gift from the gods impedes more serious discussions and investigations of this very important topic. This notion, essentially a myth in my opinion, distracts us from looking at what we as medical leaders can and should do to help guide ourselves and our colleagues. Once we put this fairytale to bed, we can then pull back the curtain and start to examine why some leaders succeed and others don't. So if leadership isn't just about a "cult of personality," what is it about? What are the key elements of leadership that matter and how can we learn to be good or even great leaders ourselves? Drucker lists several factors that we will examine one by one.

Starting off, let's make it clear that leadership is not an inherent personality trait, it is a set of actions. This is the first step in stripping away the facade and getting to the nature of leadership. As Drucker puts it bluntly, leadership is work. Breaking these tasks out, first and foremost in terms of priority is that leaders define the mission of the organizations. This encompasses the overused term, "vision" but also includes the goals and values. The mission of the organization defines boundaries—both what it will do as well as what it won't. Both are critical to successful leadership, particularly in tough times, like those that most of us in healthcare are experiencing.

This includes pushing the agenda forward so that the organization does what it needs to do. As the tiresome cliché goes, herding medical people, particularly physicians, to get them to go in the same direction can be quite challenging. Most private groups find it particularly difficult to punish their members, especially when there is a partnership or another type of ownership structure. While hard data are difficult to acquire, anecdotes from practices in my own field of radiology in the USA suggest that until quite recently, private practices rarely took the step of firing partner level employees for anything short of extreme misbehavior. Most were stable to a fault, allowing marginal or even problematic people to remain in place for anything less than a major infraction. This lowers the performance of the group and creates discord and schism within the group. Successful organizations require group cohesion and that includes enforcing group norms and values. While most leaders would prefer to use carrots, they also need to be invested with the power to sticks to succeed in this task.

Second, good leaders differ from misleaders in how they lead by their personal examples. Principled, ethical leadership includes necessary compromise—what we need to do to succeed in the real world as opposed to unprincipled behavior—whatever we can get away with, including the unethical or potentially illegal. In my own consulting work (which is primarily in the healthcare sectors), I certainly do see organizations in which the stated values (usually in a mission statement or similar document) are shared and lived by most of the practice's members. At the other extreme, I also see organizations where the stated values have nothing to do with what the practice and its members are actually doing. The mission statement in that situation is (unintentionally) laughable. At best it is ironic, but more commonly it is a sad commentary on how as individuals and organizations we can be hard at work, but not living, let alone achieving our ideals and objectives.

A related issue is that for better or worse an important, almost universal function of the leader in an organization is that of a role model. Sometimes this is aspirational, that is, people look toward leaders because they want to be become leaders themselves. When that is the case the leader has a great deal of power to set the ethical tone of the enterprise. However, even in some professional healthcare groups where there is often little interest in being the leader or where people even actively avoid leadership positions, the leader's behavior is still the most scrutinized in the group. If that person is not true to the values of the group then it is highly unlikely that anyone else will feel compelled to stay within ethical boundaries either. An ethically challenged leader can lead her or his followers into ugly or even catastrophic territory.

Even if you still aren't impressed with these arguments, there is an additional pragmatic reason that groups should try to appoint ethical leaders. People who are drawn to the healing professions for the most part have a core of idealism. They want to help others and consider their work a noble calling. They want to join other professionals and organizations where they can achieve those goals. Being a nurse, a physician, a dentist, a physician's assistant, or nurse practioner is different than most other professionals. They genuinely want to do the right thing and want to work in organizations that allow them to do the right things for their patients. While being a baggage handler is also an honest job, it doesn't share this dimension.

An important trait of organizations that succeed in the long term is coherence of goals. The people in those organizations, for the most part at least, share in the group values, goals, and mission. While that by itself won't guarantee success, it is certainly true that the opposite kind of organization rarely lasts, particularly during times of rapid change and uncertainty. If people are constantly going in different directions and fighting, the chances of success will be lower than if they can reach consensus and work together. The lack of group cohesion and commitment often leads them to flounder or fragment when the challenges hit.

In the medical field in the present times, it is more important than ever that groups are led by people who practice what they preach. Leading by example may sound old fashioned but studies of the corporate world reveal that the leaders who provide coherent, ethical leadership are the ones that are likely to create the greatest amount of long-lasting value during their tenures.

A final requirement is the necessity of personal responsibility. This is the difference between seeing a leadership position as a responsibility rather than merely a rank or a role. Again, it is not a title, a privilege or a way to isolate yourself from work or accountability. Rather, leadership is work—a set of specialized tasks that need to be done within the practice or department. Great leaders take responsibility, especially for the hard tasks and for the times when things go wrong. It is hard to summarize this point better than to quote from a relatively uncharismatic, but rather good President, Harry Truman—"The buck stops here" (the quote was used by President Truman in a plaque on his desk in the Oval Office). Blaming others, using your partners as "fall guys," pointing fingers, etc. isn't how winners lead.

## KEY POINTS

1. Understand that while charisma and "leadership skills" are important, they do not define leadership.
2. Leadership is not a position or a title, it is a set of actions. First and foremost it is work. In your organizations, make sure that you reward the work itself—providing time and resources to those who are chosen to lead.
3. Part of leadership is being a role model. Consider your actions very carefully. You have chosen a role where you can expect intense scrutiny.
4. Leaders are responsible. Shirking responsibility is one of the clearest paths to disaster. This is particularly true for elite professional organizations like healthcare group practices.

*Image credit: Woodrow Wilson (ca. 1921). Photoprint of a painting.*

# 8

# Delegation: Getting It Right to Lead Successfully

*"I not only use all the brains I have, but all I can borrow"*
—**Woodrow Wilson, American lawyer and politician, 1856-1924**
*"Get the right people in the right jobs—it is more important than developing a strategy"*
—**Jack Welch, former head of General Electric, 1935-present**

## INTRODUCTION

One of the more common limitations of medical leaders is the inability to effectively delegate. As a leader, you can err in both directions. I have seen examples of leaders who delegate too much or too little, but the latter seems to come up much more in the healthcare arena. Every leader faces the dilemma of when and why to delegate tasks to others in their organization. Even within a given task, there is a spectrum—from completely off loading a task at one extreme to letting someone do it, but maintaining close supervision at the other. No one person can or should try to run an organization by him or herself and even worse no one can effectively lead a reasonably sized organization through micromanaging. While those strategies might work in some situations, medical professionals are not usually amenable to being overly managed or "bossed." They are trained to be able to do complex jobs and expect latitude in their ability to make decisions and an element of autonomy in their positions.

These management challenges are particularly evident in medical institutions. These are often large, multimillion dollar enterprises that are facing not only the severe external pressures that we have discussed elsewhere, but also simultaneously have internal challenges as well. No outside CEO in their right mind would take on such a job in an organization like that without a clear plan to find ways to delegate both decisions and managerial tasks. It would simply be too prone to failure.

In consulting work with medical practices, I have encountered several groups that have teetered toward disaster because the president/CEO either does not want to (or can't ) delegate key administrative tasks. Just as destructive and often more common is the lack of interest by other partners in taking on these duties and roles, thus leaving it to one person usually to the detriment of all.

## DRIVERS THAT FORCE DELEGATION IN ORGANIZATIONS

Size isn't the only issue that forces leaders to delegate tasks, responsibilities, and authority. Complexity also drives the need for leaders to rely more on those they lead. The leadership and management challenges multiply quickly as organizations grow into more markets and geographies, as their goals become more diverse and as their environment changes more rapidly. The leader cannot be in all these places, let alone understand all of the markets, the personalities, the technical details, etc.

Another reason for delegation is that it is the only effective way a leader can possibly protect their ability to do their own job. Otherwise, she or he would be flooded with having to make thousands of mundane decisions each day and would be unable to do their own job of leading. The leader needs to be able to have time to focus on the larger issues that the organization is facing.

## EFFECTIVE DELEGATION

The first and perhaps the biggest task in this leadership issue of delegation is to find people you trust enough in your organization to do important tasks. They clearly need to be both reliable and trustworthy. A cliché in human resources is that you don't want people who are merely smart, but who are lazy and on the other side you also don't want people who are willing to work hard but who are not smart enough to do a good job. Rather, you need to hire people who are *both* smart and capable of meeting goals. Those are the people who can work autonomously and take on leadership challenges. These are the folks to whom you can safely delegate tasks and assignments.

When you read business books, particularly biographies, one theme that is highly consistent across most authors is this challenge. Seasoned leaders stress that the biggest hurdle to being successful is first finding the right people. If you don't have the right people, that is, if they can't do their jobs well or can't be trusted, then you can't delegate and your effectiveness as a leader will remain limited.

# EXECUTIVE DELEGATION, THE EXTREMES: CARTER AND REAGAN

Delegation is always a matter of degree. As we discussed earlier, a leader can do too much as well as too little. As a set of examples it is illuminating to consider how two recent presidents demonstrated these pitfalls in their leadership styles.

Jimmy Carter the 39th president of the USA had been a nuclear engineer by training. He came into office in 1977 in the shadow of the Watergate scandal that had led to the first resignation of a US president—Richard Nixon. His lack of experience in Washington (his previous elected position had been as governor of Georgia) was seen as a plus in the wake of public outcry over the pardon of Nixon by Gerald Ford. The public didn't appear to want another Beltway insider after such a disastrous end to a presidency. Carter had a meticulous attention to detail and remarkable ability to absorb arcane data. The problem is that isn't the job description of an executive position. Executives need to be able to manage groups of people, not just rely on their own expertise and energy. The case of the American presidency is an extreme example of this need. There is probably no other job on the planet where you are at higher risk of failure if you don't surround yourself with smart, effective people to whom you can delegate complex tasks. No job on the planet makes a bigger requirement that you need to be able to not only delegate but also to delegate to the right people and to delegate well. President Carter was criticized for most of the factors that we are discussing about delegation—poor choices of staff, inability to delegate tasks, and the impossibility of having the chief executive look at every bit of minutiae on a major decision.

President Carter's management style was lampooned in a memorable episode of the then popular variety television program "Saturday Night Live" in which the comedian playing Carter took radio call in questions from average citizens and showed a ridiculous range and depth of knowledge in answering questions, such as medical advice on how to come down from a bad recreational drug high. While the television episode was over the top, unfortunately there was some truth in the humor. He often led staff meetings that went into the weeds to go over details that should have been both delegated and relegated to other people, not the president. While Carter later denied it, White House insiders said that he would often focus on mundane tasks, such as scheduling the use of the tennis court (Fallows, 1979).

In the real world, his effectiveness and ultimately his presidency was limited by his management style. The White House couldn't adequately address the many pressing issues that arose during their 4 years. While some people excuse this by saying that he had more than his share of challenges during his term, a fair assessment is that every president has unexpected challenges.

A very telling canard about the American chief executive that we have discussed elsewhere in this book is that he or (someday) she doesn't need to go looking for trouble. In most presidential administrations, in fact, trouble, often from unexpected quarters, usually finds them. Carter's administration unfortunately was no exception, and faced a variety of serious challenges including the Soviet invasion of Afghanistan, a revolution in Iran that led to both an oil boycott and the taking of almost 100 American citizens hostage in Iran for over a year, all of that on top of a seriously ailing economy. Crises, even more so than day-to-day business, require intelligent, well-organized leadership. Like a stress test, crises expose defective leadership. They can only be handled by those with the leadership skills to rise to the occasion.

In contrast, Carter's successor, Ronald Reagan the 40th President, was also heavily criticized for his management style, but in his case it was at the other end of the delegation spectrum. He was regularly critiqued and occasionally lambasted for overly delegating his authority as the president to an inner circle of close advisors. Then President Reagan's previous career included a long history of working in radio and later in Hollywood. He was an actor and then a leader of actors, becoming the president of the Screen Actor's Guild. This background in communication and in show business gave him a strong grasp of symbolism, style, and the importance of narrative and message in the presidency. He had also been in the public political arena including being the Governor of California and when he came to Washington, he brought in an experienced crew of remarkably loyal staff and cabinet members with him from his California days. He was used to a work style where he was in charge of the command decisions, but where his advisors and staff then took care of the details without a lot of direct supervision or interference.

Upon Reagan's arrival in the White House, the press had a field day with his work style. He was not a micromanager, he didn't go deep into the technical details or wordsmith most documents. Unlike his predecessor, Mr. Carter, he would not be staying late at the office reading policy papers or managing his staff's athletic activities. Instead, he would try to be finished by 5:00 pm or so and perhaps have the Speaker of the House (at that time, Tip O'Neill, from the other side of the political aisle) over for cocktails. He often napped during the day and staff were instructed to keep meetings on time and to the point to accommodate his schedule. They apparently were under orders only to wake him for the most critical of issues. He would not have dreamed of staying up into the wee hours with his staff having college style bull sessions about policy minutiae or the budget as a subsequent president, William Clinton often did. He provided the direction for the big points and again trusted his staff both to handle the details and to execute his plans to make things happen.

The perception that he wasn't a hard worker or an involved president was serious enough. It implied that he was abdicating his role as president, creating a tier of "mini presidents" and reducing his own position to a largely ceremonial role. However a far more critical charge against his leadership style arose during his second term. When it became clear that members of his executive branch had concocted a complex arms deal that circumvented US law and the express will of the Congress, his presidency was threatened. His aides would consistently testify that while they had been involved in the machinations, the president was not in the loop. In the end both the accusation and the defense devolved into one and the same problem—that Reagan hadn't been involved because he hadn't participated in the key decisions that led to the scandal.

## GETTING DELEGATION RIGHT: THE RULES

So how can we do better as leaders when it comes to delegation. The first rule, as discussed earlier is to get the right people. You need to have people you can delegate to—they need to be able to take responsibility and you need to be able to give them latitude. You also need to make them accountable. You need to be able to tell them what to do and then let them do it. If you have to hover over them to get them to do their work and if you need to constantly check in with them to make sure that they do it right, then that really isn't delegation.

An equally important second rule is that delegation is not putting off decisions or a form of outsourcing. You, as the leader or delegator, will still need to retain some amounts of involvement, oversight, and responsibility. Some of the worst forms of leadership involve handing off responsibility to an underling, that is, "Get the ER service under control or else..." without sharing or giving the receiver of this news the authority or other tools for her or him to accomplish the task. Responsibility for a task without the authority to achieve it, particularly lone responsibility is both frustrating and stressful for the person who is nominally in charge. In the worst cases, it is also a form of nefarious leadership. The leader who doesn't want to be sullied with difficulty (or worse failure and responsibility) passes off losing tasks to underlings who can then be left shouldering that blame: "that idiot Dr. X screwed up the ER service."

The third rule is the mutual sharing of information between the leader and coworkers. One of the drivers of the need for delegation is complexity of information in your enterprise. Delegation is really a cooperative exercise and thus works both ways. You delegate because you can't know everything that your underling does and so you let her or him take charge. On the other hand, you as the leader need to share your knowledge as appropriate to help your group members be effective.

The fourth rule is that delegation is not an all or nothing event. Tannenbaum and Schmidt describe this process as a continuum with gradual devolution of more power and authority to the person or team being delegated to as they in turn demonstrate ability and competency (for more information on Tannenbaum and Schmidt Model see http://www.businessballs.com/tannenbaum.htm). This allows for a controlled transfer of power and authority and is one of the subtle keys to the art of delegation.

The fifth rule of delegation is that can also be a form of training. In the here and now, it is a way to free up more of your time and attention as a leader to focus on other issues. It also applies to the future. Smart leaders know that there will come a time when their own days of leading are numbered. For the sake of the group or department and for their personal legacy of achievement, they need to consider intelligent and effective ways to use delegation to develop the next group of leaders to take the reigns. This is not just an issue for the distant future. In my consulting work, I have advised several groups where almost all of the leadership efforts were being done by one person. All of that information was in the mind of a single brain. These groups are literally always one "plane ride" (ie, one fatal flight) or one medical catastrophe away from disaster. When most of the institutional knowledge is in the head of one person, the group is at enormous risk.

## KEY POINTS

1. Delegation is one of the defining aspects of great leadership.
2. Leaders can't just do the work themselves. They need to develop the ability to leverage their skills so that their effectiveness is multiplied.
3. Like other facets of leadership, it is not just a matter of delegating or not. You can delegate too much or too little and this determines both the effectiveness of your leadership and your group's success.

## Quarterly Report Card: Chairman of Medicine

| | |
|---|---|
| Expresses vision clearly | B+ |
| Resolves conflict | D but shows improvement |
| Manages meetings well | C |
| Delegates effectively | A |
| Works well with other departments | B |

*Image credit: Quarterly Report Card: Chairman of Medicine. © Frank Lexa*

# Making the Grade: Levels of Leadership

## INTRODUCTION

In this chapter, we will return to Jim Collin's important book *Good to Great* as part of a discussion that at times seems to be an almost forbidden topic in medical leadership. How do we classify or grade the performance of our leaders? If we claim that we understand leadership, then we certainly need to be able to distinguish great leadership from mediocre or poor leadership. We need to be able to understand when a person is leading well and when they aren't. In many healthcare institutions, it is common to see a bewildering variety of rating systems for healthcare professionals including 360 degree feedback where you are rated by people from a range of positions above and below you in the organization. Certainly the leaders, given their disproportionate effect on the success and failure of the institution need to be evaluated as well. This means grading individual leadership and when necessary separating out those who have great skills from those who don't.

This doesn't happen as frequently as it should, particularly in our field. There seem to be several reasons why we often shy away from this in medicine.

First, there seems to be a generational issue here that in our current ethos we are afraid of giving out bad grades. In some US colleges, the average grade has drifted up toward A. We have become shy about admitting that not everyone does top grade work and that by definition not every can. Distinguishing good from bad work requires an admission that there are folks out there who are below average. This applies to leadership as much as it does (or at least should) to freshman calculus classes, soccer leagues, etc.

Second, we may see it as an attack on a colleague to describe them as a mediocre leader. Fortunately (or perhaps unfortunately if this makes you uncomfortable as we discussed in the earlier paragraph), much of what leaders do can be evaluated objectively in many cases. The purpose of grading isn't merely to criticize, rather it should provide a mechanism for us to give our leaders feedback to help them improve and grow in their work. This is even more critical in leadership roles than in lesser positions.

A third reason that we may shy from evaluating our leaders is the perception that leadership is amorphous and hard to define. In another chapter, we discussed how to remove some of the mystique from leadership in order to both better understand it as well as improve performance in your organization (see also Lexa, 2008a). The trouble that many of us in medicine and science have with understanding the nature of leadership makes it difficult for us to quantify and grade. For example, in my field a radiologist who is given a grade (or a bonus) based upon how many studies she or he reads a week has a much more easily defined mechanism for being graded. Leadership isn't that simple, since it is a more complex bundle of tasks, but it can still be formally evaluated once you have more insights into what leadership means.

A fourth reason for our collective hesitancy is that depending upon your organization, implementing these measures may also include holding a mirror up to yourself. If you are in a democratic practice that elects leaders, then you as a group deserves some (or sometimes most or almost all) of the blame for choosing a poor leader and/or for failing to support them to allow them the tools that they need to succeed.

## THE IMPACT OF LEADERSHIP: THE EFFECT OF SCALABILITY

This book gives you dozens of reasons why great leadership matters and why we have been exploring it throughout these chapters. I won't repeat those here, but I do want to emphasize that one of the very interesting aspects of effective leaders is that they have disproportionate, outsize effects on the health and value of their organizations. The head of nursing has (or at least should have) much more impact on the organization than any other single nurse. If the chairman of surgery doesn't have more of an impact on the department than a junior faculty member then something is amiss in that individual leader's performance or in how her or his work role is structured. This difference in the influence of a person's work is one of the critical reasons that leadership can have great impact (for good or for ill) in an organization.

In some cases and settings, if you as an individual healthcare worker want to make more money, your value as a worker is probably relatively linear. By this I mean that for many of us, if you want to be twice as valuable to your organization you have to do about twice as much work, that is, see twice as many patients, do twice as many procedures, or give twice as many lectures, etc. In the case of clinical work, though, there are limits to human performance. You can accomplish some increase in productivity perhaps in part by working faster. There may also be some other ways that you can improve your productivity per hour by using IT tools, robots, etc. but odds are you will need to work longer hours if you want to substantially increase the amount of work that you do each day. However, a smart manager who makes decisions that improve the value of his or her organization may have scalable effects on the organization that increase value for the institution geometrically or exponentially. A leader who makes a great decision about building a new wing on the hospital (or who avoids a stupid decision about buying an expensive piece of equipment) may have an economic impact on the hospital that is several times that of what a physician or nurse contributes in the course of a year. The nature of leadership means that they have leverage that can create (or destroy…) much more value through their decisions and by making important changes in how the organization works than they do through their share of the clinical work of the institutions.

# LEVELS OF LEADERSHIP—WHAT THEY MEAN: COLLINS' CLASSIFICATION

Professor Collins has created one of the best classification schemes for leaders and what to expect from the average to the best (Collins, 2001). The lowest, a Level 1 leader is a highly capable individual making productive contributions through talent, knowledge, skills, and good work habits. Level 2 is defined as an effective team member, while Level 3 is a competent manager. The Level 4 is an effective leader, one who "catalyzes commitment" and raises performance standards. At the highest level (Level 5) is someone who can put the good of the institution ahead of their own ego to "enduring greatness."

## Limitations of Using the System in Some Institutions

One thing that has always struck me about the classification is that it is weighted toward separating out the better leaders from each other. The stratification in this system may not apply where you work. This may sound like sarcasm, but in some situations good to great may not be the range of grades that should be given out. Bad or truly awful leaders are outside the classification system since in the book it really does begin at good and then moves on to great. The first time that I saw this in business school it was displayed out of context and I had the temerity to ask if the system was extended to negative numbers. I think that my professor thought that I was being sarcastic. I wasn't (at least not that time) but I have certainly met and worked with "leaders" in medicine as well as elsewhere, who are below a 1 as it is defined on this system. This system of grading is more appropriate for some settings, because it is probably the case that the nature of the corporate system in America makes it difficult to get a CEO level job (or at least last long enough on the job for someone to include you in their business book) unless you meet some minimum standards that then start the grade scale at good.

## Putting This Into Use for Us

Ideally, we would all prefer to work with Level 5 leaders. Unfortunately, they are rare. The best leaders understand that their performance really should be measured by how well they help or hinder the group's performance rather than how they promote themselves. For many of us in medicine this may be hard to put into practice. We are trained to be high performing individuals and take on very high degrees of personal responsibility for our individual actions. Some of us are better at being team players than others. When we aren't leaders, the impact of this is variable, depending upon our work situations. The implications when we are leaders, though is crystal clear. We can't be effective in our roles unless we learn to be team players (Level 2), good managers (Level 3), effective leaders (Level 4) or best of all, true executives (Level 5).

You, as the head, may be the best healthcare practitioner in the department. You have spent decades doing this and are (rightfully) proud of both your accomplishments and your skills. However, in your role as leader, it is more important that you focus on those things that will bring out high performance in your entire team. That often means that you need to step back from clinical work to focus on managerial and leadership skills (Lexa, 2008b).

This again raises the issue of scalability. While you may be the fastest, best nurse practiner, dentist, or surgeon in your group and you can certainly work harder and better than the others on your team, the impact of working harder and longer pales in comparison with impact you can through good leadership. You can have much more impact on the group's performance if you find ways to use better management, superior IT systems, better contracts, etc. to improve the performance of ten or twenty or a hundred or more other people in the group rather than just doing more by yourself.

## BRINGING BACK GRADES: HOW DO YOU IMPLEMENT THIS?

Several years ago we reinstituted a rigorous grading system at one of the business schools where I teach. The previous system was fairly lax, with significant variability by course and department. Some courses were graded on strict curves, while others were not. The students in that class year had also voted not to disclose their grades to recruiters, and that had the effect of further diminishing the importance and impact of grading. The grades were essentially invisible to the people on which they might have had the greatest impact (job recruiting is one of the central activities and goals of MBA students). The changeover to a rigorously enforced school wide grading system on a curve was not easy to implement. It required significant adjustments both in how grading was performed and in how the data were utilized.

Some of the greatest resistance came at an emotional level. There is a tendency in elite institutions to think that once you get in, that you are great by definition and at least at some places you deserve great grades because you are great. At the extreme, there is the notion that you should get a good grade for just showing up. The evidence at some undergraduate institutions suggests that this is much more than a notion. If grade inflation pushes the average mark up into the "A" range (or it's equivalent of "outstanding," etc. in systems that have replaced letter grading with code words) then there isn't much grading going and everyone is reported out to be about the same. It was hard to push against this tendency and reinstitute grading and forced grade curves (ie, require that a distribution of grades be given, including low ones, in each class).

The same resistance to honest appraisal can be seen in some medical groups and departments as well. As professionals, we worked hard to get here. We have passed our tests with flying colors. We regularly go to meetings to continue our professional education and take recertification or maintenance of certification tests of one sort or another throughout our career. Becoming a professional is hard work and carrying the title of: physician, dentist, nurse, nurse practioner, or physician's assistant is (and should be) a well deserved honor. Aren't we all great and won't it hurt individuals to measure their performance? To judge by the gossip you hear in the hallways and after hours in some medical settings, there are clearly very active measurements going on informally in most institutions. Almost everyone seems to have an opinion (informed or not) about the performance of the leadership and how the institution should be run. However, formalized systems for evaluation seem to meet some resistance. I have been asked to review a fair number that have been implemented in healthcare and they struck me as both timid and incomplete. While these have predominately been in my own field of radiology, I have seen similar systems with similar flaws in many other medical disciplines. There are certainly some methodological flaws that limit accurate evaluation. People may feel that they aren't qualified to evaluate a leader or may be afraid to provide an honest appraisal of someone with power over them due to a fear (at times not unfounded) of retaliation. Those issues are important, but in many cases groups and departments are simply afraid to take a serious look at how their most important people were doing their jobs and just ignore the issue. However, leadership and leaders are simply too important for professionals and their organizations to ignore.

## KEY POINTS

In many of our organizations, while we all chronically evaluate our leader's decisions informally, the leader may be the last person (if at all) to be graded on a formal basis. Since no one is more important to the performance of a group or institution, good leadership (or lack thereof) requires formal review. In the next column, we will explore the characteristics of the grading systems in greater depth.

1. Make a leader's compensation tied to the group's performance.
2. Create clear goals and criteria for rewards using clearly defined grading parameters as part of the reward process.
3. Use time and schedule incentives to give a leader time to do leadership tasks.

# 10

# Educating Leaders:
# A Foundation Curriculum
# for HealthCare Professionals

*"Leaders aren't born they are made. And they are made just like anything else,
through hard work. And that's the price we'll have to pay to achieve that goal,
or any goal."*
—**Vince Lombardi, American football coach and executive in the
National Football League, 1913–1970**

## INTRODUCTION

In this book, we are exploring important issues in leadership for
healthcare leaders and their groups. This topic has come to the fore in
many fields within medicine. In my specialty, the American College of
Radiology has a Commission on Leadership and Practice Development
to address the issues in this domain. The College studied the need for
leadership training and decided to found an institute, Radiology Leadership Institute (RLI) in 2012 to both develop and hone the leadership
skills of US radiologists. This was envisioned as encompassing five levels
in leadership development, ranging from a beginning level—mastering
the issues that trainees, residents and fellows need when they are about
to enter practice from training, through the skills that mid career leaders
need in their practices and department all the way up to those that are
required for advanced leadership roles in their profession. Those encompass four sequential steps in the development of a practice leader, with a
final fifth category that is honorary for those who have made outstanding
contributions to the specialty through their leadership contributions. As
a matter of background and of disclosure, I have been deeply involved in
this work since the inception and am currently both an active educator at

Leadership Lessons for Health Care Providers. http://dx.doi.org/10.1016/B978-0-12-801866-8.00010-X

several of the levels and also recently became a board member of the RLI. In this chapter, I would like to share some aspects of this effort and the promise that it holds for radiologists and their groups. I believe that this framework can provide a useful starting point for other medical specialties and health practioner organizations that are interested in pursuing this worthy goal. In this chapter, I will focus on the common foundation that we felt that all diagnostic radiologists should have at the entry stage, Level I.

## LEVEL I: GOALS

The level I curriculum has as its purpose to create a common core of knowledge that all young practicing radiologists should share in the nonclinical realms. The purposes are several fold:

First, it will include a "business bootcamp" of subjects that radiologists need to know but do not usually cover in their medical school or residency training—graduate medical education (GME) years. For example, one segment of the curriculum will include an introduction to accounting so that as a partner in a radiology practice, you will at least be able to read a profit and loss statement and understand the salary and tax implications of group decisions. This is not to say that the learner would become an accountant, but rather that they would learn enough to be able to use accounting information at a basic level as applied to running a medical practice. This level of training will also include "must have" information for someone going out of training into their first position out of training, such as how to look at a potential practice opportunity, how to compare practices for performance and personal fit, and how to evaluate a job offer from a group or academic department.

Second, the Level I curriculum will create a shared knowledge among young physicians that should help a radiologist develop better insights into both the group dynamics and the performance and internal workings of his or her organization. This nonclinical education will provide a common language and a set of shared experiences to help create better groups and departments. One aspect of this will be an appreciation of the organizational success factors, such as good "followership," good citizenship, and strong leadership that are keys to high performing groups.

Third, while the majority of practicing diagnostic radiologists may never be a chair or a practice leader, this curriculum will also provide them their first step in that direction. It is our hope that it will not only provide training, but in the process also stimulate interest in leadership and that this training will provide a foundation on that longer journey through the higher levels of leadership. The initial proposed curriculum for this

Level I instruction for all residents in training included a series of modules which will be discussed next.

The curriculum is undergoing a process of continual improvement both to increase the specificity of each module and to provide more flexibility. The curriculum is constantly undergoing updating and review, but the listing given later provides you with a sense of what the fundamental elements contain. The coursework is now delivered in a "blended" fashion, meaning a mixture of live lectures and web-based tools. Ideally the live component should not only be substantial, but should also involve active learning and participation by the learners. The priority is to deliver talks that cover mission critical topics, such as leadership, professionalism, and others that emphasize group participation and interactivity. The venues of the courses that we give include the national meetings of the ACR in order to demonstrate the institutional commitment to the next generation of leaders and to simultaneously promote networking and mentoring in a live setting.

## CURRICULUM ISSUES

The final form of the curriculum included five levels ranging from the Level 1 (a common foundation for all members of the profession) scaling up with higher levels as the individual's career responsibilities and leadership responsibilities demand. While covering the curriculum of all the levels is out of the scope of this book, I would like to provide a suggested list of topics that can be used as a starting point. These can be adapted where necessary to other fields within medicine, but provide a good set of foundation topics for leaders in healthcare in the USA during the challenging times that we face in the second decade of the 21st century.

A suggested foundation curriculum for getting started in healthcare leadership (adapted from Lexa et al., 2011) that can be used as a starting point for you personally or for your professional organization is as follows:

1. Strategic Challenges to the Future of US Medicine
2. Introduction to Financial principles for healthcare professionals
3. Healthcare Systems: how they operate in the US (or plug in your nation here) including how they get paid in both the public and private sectors
4. CMS, RUC, wRVUs, CPT, and other acronyms you need to understand how to do coding, billing, and other bureaucratic work in healthcare
5. Negotiations 1—internal issues to your department or group

6. Negotiations 2—advanced issues for negotiations external to your group, including institutions, systems and where appropriate, political work
7. Marketing, Branding, and Promoting Health Services to the many stakeholders we serve
8. Your first job after training-getting it, getting it right, making it work, and keeping it
9. Health Care reform and change and its impact on US (or your nation's) medicine
10. Personal Career Management from Hiring to Retirement—how to manage your career, insights from successful leaders
11. Service and Quality Issues in Healthcare—putting patients at the center of high quality healthcare while meeting mandates from institutions and organizations
12. Service and Quality Issues in Healthcare—other medical professionals, administration, and other stakeholder groups
13. Professionalism in healthcare—staying true to your values and the oath you took when you decided to become a healthcare professional
14. Leadership—personal and local issues
15. Leadership—interacting with larger organizations and building influence outside your organization(s)
16. Accounting practices for medical professionals—what you need to know
17. Macroeconomics 101—why the dismal science matters to healthcare leaders and (at a minimum) what they need to know
18. What makes a medical group great and how to foster superior group dynamics and success in your group or department
19. Strategic planning for medical leaders—why this alien sounding topic has become so important for us
20. Envisioning the future of healthcare-learning to anticipate change in the public and private sectors.

The aforementioned curriculum can be adapted to the diverse sectors in healthcare that all of us work within in order to make it specific and germane to our specific fields. While there are certainly other topical areas that can be added in to address specific areas of leadership concerns that are specific to your field of nursing, emergency medicine, being a hospitalist, etc. almost all of us in healthcare, regardless of our role can benefit from a smart, forward thinking nonclinical education that focuses on the fundamentals.

## KEY POINTS

1. Organizations throughout healthcare will succeed (or fail) based on the participation of their membership in leadership roles.
2. The proposed Level I curriculum will provide a starting point for developing a common leadership foundation for healthcare professionals.
3. While the Level I was created for a single medical specialty, it can be adapted fairly easily to a wide variety of types of healthcare workers and professionals.
4. Leadership development is the key for our future in these challenging times.

*Image credit: © Frank Lexa*

# 11

# Learning to Lead: Best Practices for Getting Started

*"Tell me and I'll forget; show me and I may remember; involve me and I'll understand."*
—**Chinese Proverb**

## INTRODUCTION

In the previous chapter, we discussed how to get started in learning to be a leader, including the proposed entry, level I, training of the Radiology Leadership Institute (Lexa et al., 2011). This discussion was focused on the "what." If you only have a limited amount of time (pretty much the description of most of us who work in the healthcare sector today) what should the core curriculum of a nonclinical program in basic leadership skills look like. These types of topics are important to all of us in healthcare and can certainly be adapted to other types of professionals outside healthcare such as engineers, chemists, etc. You have already taken an important step on your leadership journey by reading this far into the book. Now we will discuss both the "how" of how to acquire that training and cover that curriculum. You have options in how to pursue your education. We will also move past the basics and then discuss how to build upon that foundation and develop the more advanced real world abilities, training and personal skill sets and assets that a successful leader needs.

## HOW TO LEARN WITH A FORMAL CURRICULUM

Before moving on to other types of leadership training, let us start by addressing the issue of how to deliver the core leadership curriculum. In the digital age, there is a near constant discussion at major business

Leadership Lessons for Health Care Providers. http://dx.doi.org/10.1016/B978-0-12-801866-8.00011-1

schools of the role of residential or "face to face" classroom education versus synchronous or asynchronous forms of online learning as well as innovative ways to deliver content in novel interactive ways. While digital tools are heavily used at major institutions, there is a highly consistent point of agreement among the business schools where I teach regularly. Why there are many points of controversy and much ongoing experimentation and analysis, for now there is a consensus that the curriculum must be both active and interactive in order to be effective. This is true whether you do it face to face or online, whether live or asynchronous. As the Chinese proverb that opened this chapter points out, there is a substantial gulf separating merely listening to a lecture versus learning through doing. Just reading a book or watching a webcast is not adequate for teaching the major topics that are at the heart of the leadership curriculum that we laid out in the previous chapter. Subjects such as professionalism, leadership, or strategy can't really be learned by memorizing a set of bullet points and then answering a set of true/false questions.

Merely attending a live lecture, doesn't count as an interactive experience by itself. If the learner is passively sitting in their seat counting the minutes to the lunch break, then the impact is likely to be very low. The difference that I noted when I shifted from medical school lecturing to the business school classroom teaching in the early 2000s was striking. At the medical school, I did not take attendance, I was not allowed to call on students and I brought enough slide material to cover the entire period except for a short 5 min or so at the end to allow the students to ask me questions. The only parts that were interactive were the voluntary questions at the end to me and the questions that I submitted for the final examination.

In contrast, when we lecture to our students, business school professors not only take attendance, but also call out to the class for answers and furthermore call on specific students if they are not participating. The students have a name card in front of them to facilitate this process. Class participation is not only required but also graded. In the classes that I taught in Spain, the student's class participation counts for almost half their final grade. It is also often the determining factor in their grades since it is much more variable in quality than their papers and other graded efforts.

For the topics that we put into the leadership curriculum there is much more substantial impact from learning by doing. By contrast, if you are watching a core lecture then just tackling a short set of multiple choice questions at the end doesn't count as making it a truly interactive experience. Is the ability to answer a simplistic question like the following indicative of a successful leadership program?

Which of the following is the best way to motivate your healthcare workers?

**A.** Monetary rewards for clinical productivity
**B.** Public humiliation
**C.** 360 degree feedback while setting group norms
**D.** Floggings as needed.

While the obvious answer is D (just kidding—the least worst answer is C, but none of them are great, effective motivation often requires several simultaneous strategies), the nature of leadership is that the answers are rarely simple. Instead, nuance, context and ambiguity dominate how a leader makes a good decision. While other tests in our professional life and elsewhere may have simple, relatively unambiguous answers like: "IV epinephrine-stat," Harrisburg, 42, etc., leadership topics are much complicated—more like an essay question than a fill in the blank or multiple choice test.

Leadership education is much richer if it captures the complexity and richness of leadership decision as opposed to the reductionism that I was lampooning previously. Helping people to become better leaders is a different type of education. It requires dialog and an iterative process of building the discussion to be effective. Classroom learning can be highly effective, but only if it is challenging to students. In the business world, this is often called a "coproduction" model of learning. Both the professor and the classroom participants are actively involved in the teaching process. The students bring their experience into the classroom and actively participate in problem solving. They work through issues of complexity, nuance, and ambiguity. Potential leaders need to understand that a checklist or set of bullet points about leadership is a starting point, not a culmination of leadership training.

For you as potential leaders, understand that there are proven methods for doing this and that it will take time with experienced leaders who are capable of teaching this face to face to accomplish the formal curriculum. Be very wary of those who claim that leadership can be distilled into a quick cookbook recipe. Like learning to speak passable Mandarin in 7 days or making millions in day trading in your basement from your personal computer these simplifications are at best foolish and at their worst they are damaging scams.

## SEMINARS, DURABLE LECTURES, AND OTHER MATERIALS

While your foundation curriculum should be mostly interactive, it doesn't follow that every learning experience needs to be intensely collaborative. Just as you may do your periodic review CME on the web as part of a personal study program, there are many great seminars, books, and DVDs that focus on the business aspects of healthcare, including leadership. I would include a list here, but since I have participated in many of them I will avoid the appearance of a conflict. Even more informally, it is a good idea to aim to regularly read business and leadership books and to habitually read periodicals and news sources that other leaders rely upon. These include the top newspapers in the US and elsewhere, and magazines, such as the Economist, Foreign Affairs, and other highly regarded sources. This isn't a complete list but just to suggest some reliable starting points for you.

Now that we can reflect on several decades of experience with the internet, it is safe to say that there is no shortage of available information, nor is there a shortage of people willing to opine upon it. The real problem is the opposite—a deluge of information of diverse levels of quality including misinformation and disinformation. To say it another way, the challenge for leaders isn't a paucity of data, rather it is a shortage of wisdom. Wisdom would allow them to filter out the noise and misinformation so that they can get to the best, actionable information and the most trenchant analysis. Much of the publically available information is poorly researched or simply wrong. Given the prevalence of psychiatric disease, it isn't surprising that with billions of people who have access to connected computers that there is a lot of misinformation, junk, and even insanity on the web. Always start your education with quality sources and maintain a critical stance both with them and those that you branch out to. As one of my teachers put it in the predigital age, read the good books first and you won't have time to waste on the bad ones. In our digital era, go to the quality websites and other resources first. You won't run out of them and you won't have time to waste on the poor quality sites.

## MENTORSHIP

Not all leadership training and development occurs in a classroom or seminar session. Some of the best training occurs one on one with role models in an apprenticeship or mentorship relationship. Finding the right mentor(s) is one of the tasks a leader needs to accomplish. That person or better those persons (most of us, including myself, need more than one mentor) can help guide you and assist you as you progress through your career. It is also a reminder of two more key issues. First, that leadership development never stops. Your growth as a leader depends upon challenging yourself and seeking training beyond the foundation. You will be challenged throughout your time as a leader and the answers are not going to be in a textbook, in a presentation or even on the web. Having a trusted friend who can counsel you with their experience is priceless. Second, leaders need to be mentors themselves. This is important for them and for their mentees. You will learn a lot about leadership through mentoring a younger colleague and you will also be aiding the next generation in the same way that you were once helped. This is part of your legacy and also completes a virtuous circle, tying generations together.

## BUILDING A NETWORK

Another important form of informal leadership development and growth is to build a network of more informal relationships to help you with day to day challenges. Leaders need an address book of people that they can call on for advice and help. One of the legacies of my business school experience is that now, over a decade later, we contact each other more than ever to help each other with everything from advice to getting access to companies and key people. This should be a lifetime process of building friendships and professional relationships to help you through good times and bad. You will need good networks in order to succeed in your career. Start building them now, even if you don't feel that you need them—you will whether you become a leader or not.

## KEY POINTS

1. Your core educational curriculum should be interactive, challenging you and delivered live by world class leaders in your profession.
2. A foundation curriculum is just that, a starting point. Dedicate yourself to building upon that foundation.
3. Mentorship is at the heart of great leadership. You should seek out mentors and actively mentor others. This should start at the beginning of your professional life, even during your training.
4. Build a strong network of people you can rely on for advice and help through every stage of your career.

**Steps in Effective Teamwork from a leader's perspective:**

1) Lead a group in extensive discussions

2) Let everyone air their views

3) Decide that the leader is right

*Image credit: Steps in Effective Teamwork from a leader's perspective © Frank Lexa*

# 12

# Leadership—Organizational Styles and Types

*"I am the decider in chief"*
—*George W. Bush, 43rd President of the United States, 1946-present*

*"Team work is a group of people doing what I tell them to do"*
—*T-shirt slogan seen in 2009 in Ocean City, New Jersey*

## INTRODUCTION

If you look in the business section of a library or a bookstore (if you can still find one of those) you will quickly see that it is usually packed with tomes that address the role of leaders in organizations. If you look in the subsection of books on business biography that is a particularly crowded sector that usually focuses on leadership aspects of business success. However, despite the large number of books, the advice they offer isn't easy and the answers are at times contradictory and even bewildering. Going past a quick perusal, a detailed analysis shows that the messages and conclusions of these analyses are often in conflict. On one side are books that emphasize the key role of the alpha leader in guiding the group—often promoting a clear, pyramidal command structure. In those books, he or she takes the lion's share of the credit for the success of the company. At the other extreme, are works that downplay the role of the leader in providing command and control functions and instead extol the distributed nature of knowledge and power and the virtues of a "flat" nonhierarchical organization. In that type of organization, the leader has more of a "guru" or "vision" role rather than day to day tactical duties, but again may receive the lion's share of the credit for creating and guiding such an organization.

Neither extreme is actually very common in large companies in day to day practice in the 21st century, instead many firms have a blended form of leadership lying somewhere in the middle of the spectrum rather than at the endpoints. Understanding that there is more than one kind of style

Leadership Lessons for Health Care Providers. http://dx.doi.org/10.1016/B978-0-12-801866-8.00012-3

(and that there are diverse paths to success) is a good starting point in your leadership training. People are different and not unexpectedly leadership styles, particularly preferred leadership styles can vary quite a bit. Whether you are a leader now, a future leader, or just someone who wants to help your group to succeed, it is important to understand the role that these leadership styles and the organizational structures around you can play in the success or failure of a medical group or department.

To start this exploration, we need to understand that much of the time the leadership style and the organizational structure are reasonably in sync. If a leader has been around for a while and is doing his/her job well, it is not unusual for he or she to consciously or unconsciously adapt to the organization and vice versa with the organization either adapting or being adapted to the leader's will and style. It is when institution and the leader aren't a good match that the drama ensues. That is usually an unstable situation—either the organization changes or the leader changes or conflict will arise. When that doesn't resolve quickly, the mismatch can become fairly dysfunctional and sooner or later there will be a regime change.

While the categories that we will explore later in this chapter are good starting points, it is also important to understand that many organizations have more than one style and/or they don't fit easily into a single category. Another caveat is that we also need to be clear that organizational diagrams, job titles, and roles rarely tell the whole story of how a group or institution functions. An organization may describe itself as democratic and flat in the hierarchical sense because that is the aspiration of the people who wrote the vision statement, but like descriptions on internet dating sites, it may not be a completely accurate description of the truth. There are often significant differences between the "nominal" way that an organization describes itself and how it actually works—who really calls the shots, who do people go to with problems, how do conflicts actually get resolved, etc. Is the leader really the leader or are there other people who actually make the important decisions? Does the leader have an enormous blind spot, that is, he/she thinks that they are a benign, guru leader while people who work under them see them as rigid, authoritarian micromanagers.

A very important part of being a good leader is the ability to read the situation (social IQ if you will) to understand how to get things done in circumstances like those described previously. You also need to be able to do a better job than most of us in reducing your personal blind spot and understanding the issues of blind spots and cognitive dissonance in individuals and organizations. In the end, truth will usually win and those who are more realistic will be better leaders for their pragmatic realism.

Regardless of your individual style, the soft power issues that drive organizational dynamics need to be clearly understood if you are to lead successfully in any size group. To make the point stronger, that dissonance between nominal and actual power structures has become standard fare for Hollywood's comedic depictions of corporate and military organizations. In these movies and television shows, nominal leaders are often buffoonish and downright stupid while nonleaders are actually the conduits for getting things done. While this may seem exaggerated for comedic or dramatic effect, the underlying narrative has some truth to it. While people may have titles and positions, the organization's actual channels of power and its effectiveness are not infrequently quite different. In the real world, it is important to understand that organizations and their leadership can have significant stylistic variations. One size does not fit all and there is genuine diversity in those who succeed as well those who struggle and fail. Next, we will examine some common styles of leadership and organization.

## AUTHORITARIAN ORGANIZATIONS: THE GOOD, THE BAD, AND THE UGLY

Authoritarian organizations are at the extreme of an interesting comparative tool called the Hofstede Personal Distance Index (Hofstede, 1983). These are top down organizations where decisions are made by a small group or even a single leader. Orders for action (at least the important issues) are delivered from on high and are then implemented below by the underlings. At the extreme, orders are carried out with little thought and with limited feedback of information from the bottom to the top. While popular with dictators, megalomaniacs, and extreme narcissists, this is rarely the blueprint for the long-term success of organizations that have to live in the real world of the 21st century. The structural flaws of these types of institutions are particularly apparent in knowledge organizations. Most of us in healthcare are working in knowledge organizations, where the key employees are highly trained professionals who are drawn to intellectual challenges. These people don't like being treated like drones and they lose their value to the organization if you put them into jobs that don't allow them to do what they do best—using their minds to solve interesting problems.

The lack of high quality, real time information flowing back up to the leader almost always creates significant impediments to speedy, accurate decision making. This is also almost never the way that groups of sophisticated professionals like physicians, nurses and other medical professionals, engineers, and scientists function. Groups of knowledge workers are much more effective if they can utilize the strengths of information and opinions from many of the levels in the hierarchy. This can be seen in many ways; one of the most striking is the architecture of knowledge worker's office space. The use of open meeting spaces, flexible collaboration space and deliberate inclusion of coffee bars and other nodes for spontaneous meeting all promote knowledge sharing. Collaboration is inhibited by closed office doors. Leaders of knowledge workers should leverage the strengths of highly trained professionals by encouraging collaboration and communication rather than isolating, ignoring or discounting their contributions.

That observation though doesn't negate the fact that centralization of decision making still manages to lurk in many of our institutions. While having a pharaoh or tsar-like leader at the top may seem hopelessly outdated, there are often strong authoritarian tendencies in larger institutions as we go through the middle of the second decade of the 21st century. This also includes those institutions in healthcare, even where the vision and the mission statement and organizational chart would suggest otherwise. Like the T-shirt slogan that opened this chapter, there is sometimes more than a little cognitive dissonance between what we would like to believe about our organizations and how we actually behave within them.

For other reasons, the pyramidal structure described earlier is almost never the actual structure for a healthcare practice. For an incoming department chair, if many of the faculty are tenured that leaves the new leader with little leverage over either the faculty members' day to day performance, let alone their employment status. In a private practice setting, the CEO or President of a small to medium sized medical group may have little or no ability to order other partners to do things, let alone be able to do something as extreme as fire a partner. This can create enormous frustration for a leader who has responsibility for an organization's performance but yet lacks the authority that she or he needs to succeed. The ability to decide who should be part of a team, a department or a hospital or university is a huge factor in the success or failure of an institution. If you can't get the right people and if you cannot put in places measures to help the wrong people become the right people, then you are sitting on a giant liability. You may not be able to successfully lead in that situation.

In fact for many leaders I have consulted within healthcare, this is their biggest challenge. In many of the bestsellers of the business literature, the book's title, or at least the first chapter or two, usually describes the most important key to success as getting the right people in your team. For many of us, we are handed the team and have limited ability (at least in the short term) to change the composition of our team.

While it may surprise some readers, there do seem to be circumstances, where a "benign" dictatorship or mildly authoritarian style seems to be not quite so noxious to some healthcare professionals. For some healthcare workers, it is preferable to be able to focus on their craft and leave the "bureaucratic" or "business" details to a chairperson or president/CEO who gravitates toward the role and hopefully also shows a flair for management tasks and skills. The latter may work in some circumstances, but understand that you as a professional can't have it both ways. If you as a professional abdicate from personal activity in doing leadership work and participation in key functions, such as practice building, contracting, promoting the practice and other decisions and then appoint someone else to do those duties, then you had better hope that your "dictator" is both benign and effective. You cannot delegate all of those executive functions and then turn around and spend most of your work time undermining and second-guessing the person trying to do them. That is a prescription for dysfunction and ending up with the worst of both worlds: a dictatorship that performs badly or not at all.

## DEMOCRACY AND ITS DETRACTORS

While private independent medical practice has been on the decline in recent years in the United States (see Jacob, 2014), this still represents an important component of healthcare delivery. Many free standing medical practices are at least relatively democratic and often quite egalitarian. The partners tend to participate in and vote on many or most of the key issues facing the practice. While a smaller group of leaders or committees may investigate issues and craft proposals, the most important issues are usually required to be put to a group vote of a leadership council or in many cases all of the partners with voting privileges. The advantage of this structure is that there is full participation—at least of the partner/owners of the practice. Everyone's voice can be heard and important information can be brought in front of the group. This resonates well with our sense of participation in a democratic society and the egalitarian precepts of a participant owned organization (as opposed to merely being an employee of company).

There are downsides though and some people have characterized this dark side as the "pathology" of democracy that we have discussed earlier. The leader's style is often that of the clichéd "cat herder" with some responsibility, but not enough authority to match that responsibility. If a significant percentage of the group doesn't participate in leadership roles and doesn't have an interest in the real issues the leaders face, but they still come to the partners meetings to oppose the leader's decisions, that can cause enormous anger and frustration for leaders trying to do the right thing for the group. Furthermore, it can also become a recipe for stalemate. Being a minority party without an alternative agenda or without ideas is mere oppositionalism and leads to stalemate and impotence. Depending upon the group's by-laws regarding whether a simple majority or a super majority vote is required for major decisions, factions may be able to fight ad nauseum with each other and create stasis. In some times and places that might not be disaster, but these are not those times. Times of great change and challenge require intelligence, decisiveness, speed, and resilience. An alternative state of stupidity, indecision, sluggishness, and rigidity is a pretty accurate recipe for not just failure but extinction.

For knowledge organizations, at the group level, participatory democracy thrives and succeeds with informed, involved participants. The effective leader pulls in diverse viewpoints and ideas then marshals the group's support, and effectively builds consensus. In the case of medical practices and organizations, if the majority of the members is actively involved in the organizational functions of the group and well informed on the issues then those meetings are likely to be highly productive and the effectiveness of their input will add value to the work of the leaders rather than obstruct their efforts.

## EXECUTIVE STRUCTURES: REPUBLICAN GOVERNMENT

In a representative, republican (with a small "R") form of leadership, the members hand over the responsibility for all or most of the key decisions to their chosen leaders. There are often specific constraints on which decisions require a full group vote versus which can be carried out by the leadership, that is, an expenditure over a certain size or an important personnel change would require all the partners to participate rather than just the leadership. As practices grow in size, it becomes harder for all the partners to participate in every meeting and decision. When you were a group of five internists serving a single hospital, you probably were able to see each other just about every day you were all in town and talk through most of the issues the group faced. In those circumstances, you were/are often able work out most of the key decisions effectively with informal leadership and management, come to a consensus that you can all live with and carry it out. However, by the time you are covering multiple sites over a large geography with 50 members or so, then it will be close to impossible to even get everyone in the same room for lunch, let alone imagine reaching a reasonable consensus on the tough, divisive issues.

At that size and scope, more formal leadership structures are necessary. Part of this can be accomplished using committees with defined domains (see Muroff, 2004). Part of this also needs to be an understanding that if we appoint leaders, we also need to give them the power to make decisions. It is pointless to ask them to sit in their offices and make good plans, but then have to wait for our monthly or worse quarterly or annual meeting to see if we will vote to support the decision.

As groups grow in size and the complexity of their organizations increases, the most basic forms of group democracy—the four surgeons or three dentists solving all their problems over a quick Monday morning breakfast becomes untenable when the group becomes 20 or 40 or more.

As some members take on the leadership roles, for them to be effective and the group to succeed, the leader or leaders need to be given the authority (and often formal training) to carry out decisions rapidly and decisively.

## KEY POINTS

1. There is no one type of leadership or organizational structure in private practice in healthcare. Understanding which type of leader and organization you have is a first step in understanding how to thrive.
2. There is often a significant disconnect between the stated way an organization is structured and how it actually works. You have to pay attention to both the nominal and actual if you are to succeed as a leader and/or participant.
3. Types of leadership in organizations have their pros and cons. In each case, consider both the opportunity to change the structure of the organization and how to best optimize the function of your organization's type.

*Image credit: Flight Instruments; Wikimedia Commons*

# 13

# Strategic Leadership: Setting Priorities

*"Strategy without tactics is the slowest route to victory. Tactics without strategy is the noise before defeat."*
—**Sun Tzu, The Art of War**

## INTRODUCTION

So far in this book, we have explored the nature of good (and bad) leadership in healthcare. We have covered many aspects of why leadership is effective versus ineffective. In this chapter, we will now turn to examine one of the key challenges to great leadership—your ability (or lack thereof) to correctly prioritize your strategic and tactical work and then focus on the things that matter most. While this is a challenge for any leader, it seems to be one of those things that can be a particular issue for some healthcare workers in leadership roles. Part of this may come from our perfectionist nature. We are trained in a culture where we try hard to never make a mistake. This creates the notion that everything is important and worse that everything is equally important.

Leadership is a murkier, more difficult enterprise with many (although perhaps not 50) shades of gray. People who are trained in healthcare— may be tempted to defer, delay, or ignore issues that they can't address in a "perfect" way. As Sun Tzu wrote over 2500 years ago, if we don't use strategy to make our decisions we will just be wasting both our time and efforts on an inevitable pathway to defeat. In this chapter's discussion, we will focus on why strategic goals and priorities are difficult for medical leaders and how we can all do better in setting them and carrying them out.

Leadership Lessons for Health Care Providers. http://dx.doi.org/10.1016/B978-0-12-801866-8.00013-5

## SETTING THE BIG STRATEGIC GOALS

Starting at the beginning, I will proffer a criticism—that many current healthcare leaders are not sophisticated strategists—certainly not as good at least as people who lead in some other fields. In contrast, the good news is that many of us in the medical arenas are, however, often very good at tactics. Give us a challenging patient and we can rise to the occasion, break the case down into what is important and what isn't sorting out what to do first and what to handle later. We can do a detailed history and physical. We will order the right diagnostic tests and then give a robust differential and provide important insights so that we can take excellent care of the patient. Then make it tougher by telling us that we can't do a particular test because the patient has a history of renal failure and we can come up with clever alternative plan to still get a precise answer for the patient despite that handicap.

But if you instead ask us for a comprehensive strategy for making fundamental changes in our practice in order to work effectively in a brand new accountable care organization, we might be stumped and worse perhaps even freeze up. A big part of leadership (especially the best leadership) is dealing with the unknown. Everyday you encounter issues that you didn't hear about during school. Going back to our analogy at the beginning of this book, it is analogous to leading people to the next island or over the horizon when you don't know exactly what is over there. With the ACO example, this is a challenge that you haven't faced before. ACOs didn't exist when we were in nursing training or in medical school or internship, so we don't have a ready plan for this. We are perhaps apprehensive about looking stupid or making a poor decision. Medical professionals may also be inhibited by their perfectionism as well as by exactly that sense of ambiguity that leadership sometimes entails. And yet, these are unfortunately (or perhaps fortunately) precisely the kinds of challenges that we often need to address first and foremost as we lead ourselves and our groups into the future.

In one of his many great articles, Peter Drucker defined the role of the CEO to look outside the organization to "define the meaningful Outside of the organization" (Drucker, 2004). This has always struck me as one of the best descriptions of what it means to be an apex leader. While we tend to see our leaders as working within an organization, managing the people, setting the priorities that is not the whole job, particularly for those in the C-suite, such as the CEO. She or he has an additional job, in many situations the most important one. They need to be able to scan the horizon and develop a robust strategic analysis of the threats and opportunities as well as all the other key factors in your environment. For healthcare, that "meaningful Outside" includes our payers, regulators, competitors, the various levels of government, as well as long list of other important and sometimes critical elements. At times this may seem overwhelming, but as Drucker says, the CEO is the link between the inside and outside of the organization.

## GETTING BETTER AT PLANNING

At the start, the obvious, but perhaps not so easy solution to the deficiency in our abilities in the realm of planning is to start to plan to improve your capabilities. You need to dedicate time to address your need to develop the skills in order to be able to create strategies, build plans, and set priorities. As one starting point, the use of scenarios and strategic planning in healthcare has been discussed by this author and others (see Lexa and Chan, 2010; Gill et al., 2005; Enzmann et al., 2011). The interested reader is referred to those sources for a more detailed discussion of this process. As you become more interested in the topic, those resources can lead you to some of the more accessible primary literature on these subjects and perhaps also stimulate you to attend live training sessions and workshops in strategy, tactics, and planning offered by the leaders of your professional organization. This training will help you to clarify what you think you need to prepare for in the future and then that should bring your priorities into focus. Remember that you will need to personalize this. It won't be enough to use the strategic analysis of a think tank, your major professional organization, or another group of professionals like you. Those types of tools can give you a huge head start and will certainly help you avoid missing a big, nasty element of the future. But always remember that strategy and tactics need to be applied locally. As the legalese at the end of a financial or dietary supplement commercial often says—"your results may be different." What worked in a surgical service at a VA hospital in California may give you insights into what to do in your primary care clinic in Maine, but always adapt your plan to your local circumstances and maintain a flexible and resilient approach to how you carry out a plan.

## SO I KNOW WHAT TO DO AS A LEADER, WHY CAN'T I GET IT DONE?

Next is the problem of having too much to do and not having the time resources for the job of leading. In my consulting work with medical practices in the United States, I meet lots of very smart, very dedicated physician leaders, nursing leaders, and other healthcare professional medical leaders as well as many other types of business leaders who are in utterly different sectors than those that we inhabit in healthcare. They have read the literature, they have often done a bit of leadership training of one kind or another, and they already know most what they think that they need to do in order to be an effective leader. The missing piece for many of them is that either their group won't give them the time to do the job and/or they can't or won't put the time into the work in order to do it well. Being a health professional is demanding job, period. Then being the leader of US$50–100,000,000 per year company on top of that is yet another demanding job. Doing both would require about 120 h a week for most of us to do well, perhaps requiring more than a touch of mania and/or sleep deprivation in order to be able to keep at it.

As a leader, you need to be smart enough to first manage yourself well and then to manage your group's expectations so that you have the resources you need. In over 10 years of doing this, I don't think that I have seen a private practice group yet where the medical leader was given *too* much time off the clinical schedule to fulfil their nonclinical duties. In fact, the opposite is more the norm. When I sit down across from the leader in that sad state of affairs, I can often see in the first 15 min that he/she is on a path to burnout or in at least a case or two already there. They aren't just tired, they are also frustrated with their inability to accomplish their goals. A highly trained nurse practitioner or dentist or any of the rest of us in healthcare usually has very high personal standards. They like to perform at high level and most of us hate to lose or to fail. These leaders are also not uncommonly angry at their group both for not supporting them and then for not appreciating their efforts. Many of them suffer from the classic conundrum of having more responsibility than authority. They get blamed for things that they often don't have the power or the times or other resources to really address. As a friend of mine who was on his own path to burnout put it both bluntly and sadly, using a comment that I had heard more from people who work in politics in Washington: "you don't become a chairman to make friends. If you want a friend, Frank, get a dog."

Keep in mind that in most good leadership positions, you don't just fill a slot, you need to actually craft the position and make it your own. In another chapter, we have discussed in detail many of the things that a leader needs to do to strategically manage their time. I can't emphasize enough how important this is for any leader, but particularly for one who is juggling leadership duties with clinical responsibilities (and in many settings also teaching, research, and other important obligations).

## LEADERSHIP AND OTHER OPEN-ENDED KNOWLEDGE WORK

One of the frustrating things for many physician leaders is the open ended, amorphous nature of the job. Unlike working a double hospital shift or a stint in the ED, leadership doesn't involve a patient list-limited nor a time-limited work shift. In one sense, it is fair to say that it is never done. It can follow you outside the normal time and space limits of your clinical work. You have a responsibility to yourself to set the limits (if necessary) of your duties as a leader. Carrying a pager, or in a more up to date example, being available electronically 24/7 can be a path to ruin. Setting limits, developing work/life strategies that keep you sane, and developing intelligent practices for delegation will all help. At a more profound level, you will also have to come up with processes to figure out what your job is and how to do it. This is probably much more nebulous than many of the other roles that you trained for as a medical professional. We will close with a couple of pieces of advice about how to handle this.

First, once you have set your goals and priorities from your strategic work, ask yourself if you have set them too high or too low. Also, understand that most of us try to develop a diversified portfolio of goals that includes both the big hard goals, such as: "we will revamp this department and make this the premier oncology center in the tri-state area" as well as some that are more limited and focused, that is, we will increase our academic output or we will improve our conferences with the neurology department.

Second, on a week to week or day to day basis you should continue to prioritize. Go back to our discussion in Chapter 5 about the matrix that distinguishes urgent and nonurgent and important and not so important along two axes. Ask yourself if you are focusing on the important issues or are you getting too caught up in minutiae. Some things like the new wallpaper in the waiting room just aren't that important, particularly for a harried leader. In addition, some of us are deliberately distracting themselves. I worked once with an important leader who was faced with a major personnel crisis. He spent hours looking at carpet samples for a conference room makeover as a way of diverting his attention from a very difficult predicament that really required his full attention.

To build on the material in Chapter 5, some people find it helpful to map their "to do" lists into a $2 \times 2$ matrix of urgent versus routine and display that against important versus unimportant. The resulting four categories then devolve into two interesting and two uninteresting categories. The latter are the unimportant and nonurgent (cleaning up your desk drawers, which you may be able to successfully put off until you retire) and the obviously urgent and important, such as putting out fires, like an angry physician who thinks that your staff made a bad choice last night on a VIP who was admitted through the ED with complex symptoms. These are both easy from a strategic perspective—you usually can't ignore the ones that are urgent and important and ignoring the nonurgent and unimportant is the right thing to do unless you have a remarkable amount of free time.

The more interesting categories are the remaining two and they are often the ones that distinguish smart strategists from the amateurs. We let ourselves get distracted by things that are unimportant but are "urgent." These are often the kinds of priorities that are urgent to someone else, but not to you and are really of low importance to you and your group. The final category is the hardest one for many leaders. This category—the important thing that may make or break your group, but doesn't have to be handled this minute, is often the one that we procrastinate over and consequently miss an opportunity. Try to push yourself into taking care of these or perhaps at least whether they deserve your attention. Keep in mind that a great leader can't do everything so make sure to reevaluate this from time to time.

## KEY POINTS

1. Strategic thinking and planning is a critical task for a leader. If you ignore this, you are leaving one of your most important, perhaps the most important work undone. This is analogous to focusing on rearranging the deck chairs while the Titanic sinks under the waves.
2. Seek out formal training and advice when you are figuring out what the future may hold.
3. Make sure that you have the resources from your group and from yourself to be the leader that you want to be. Well-intentioned failure is still failure. Trying your hardest at impossible job and failing is still failure. Be smart enough to anticipate that trap and figure out ways to change things so that success is possible.
4. Understand that your time as a leader is a valuable resource. Get the important things done and continually reevaluate what is really important.

*Image credit: Cuckoo clock, so-called Jagdstueck, Black Forest, ca. 1900, Deutsches Uhrenmuseum Furtwangen; Wikimedia Commons*

# Time to Lead

*"It is not enough to be busy. So are the ants. The question is: What are we busy about?"*
—*Henry David Thoreau, writer and philosopher, 1817–1862*

## INTRODUCTION

For those of us in the medical fields, whether we are leaders or not, it seems that there is never enough time. We try to balance our work duties with our home lives, juggling tasks left and right, often without great success. In a medical practice, this dilemma is compounded if you also have leadership responsibilities in addition to your clinical tasks. For many of leaders in our field, the expectation seems to be that you should carry a demanding clinical load and also be able to do managerial and leadership tasks. In my own career I have worked outside of medicine at times and when I do am always struck by how much more seriously both those people and also their organizations take their leadership responsibilities. Both the individuals and their companies have a greater respect for the time demands that good leadership requires. They understand that leadership is the job, not a component or afterthought. Being the head of a company that does 50 million dollars a year in revenue is a full time (and often far more than a full time) job. Yet in some medical settings, too often we seem to expect that our leaders should also carry her or his share of the clinical work or do other nonleadership tasks, despite the fact that our medical enterprises are often in that size range and many times are at least as complex in their leadership requirements as those in a nonmedical corporation.

This is a serious cultural disconnect in healthcare that you need to address at both a personal level as a leader and also as a member of a group or institution. It is no fun to fail and in particular it is no fun to fail in a leadership role. Failure in leadership will likely make you depressed and will probably hinder your future efforts both by making you cautious and because many leaders fail in public and the public has a long memory for

Leadership Lessons for Health Care Providers. http://dx.doi.org/10.1016/B978-0-12-801866-8.00014-7

your failures. In this chapter, we will explore the specifics of how and why you should set aside time in order to be a successful leader.

## TIME OFF THE CALENDAR

A portion of your work as a leader—some of the leadership tasks at least—is predictable. If you are fortunate, you can schedule all your major meetings with the hospital administration on a particular day of the week in afternoon and perhaps also use some of that block of time for "office hours" or for having an open door policy with their fellow professionals, technical staff, and other people who need access to you. If things are quiet, you may even be able to work on budgets, do planning, and many of the other core tasks of leading and managing a group in that same time slot. That kind of protected regular time off of the clinical schedule is necessary for many medical practice or department heads and provides a base or floor to your time commitment as a leader. It is not enough, but it is a start. Conversely, not having that time and then regularly trying to drop your other duties and then leave the hospital wards or your clinic for meetings will degrade both your clinical performance and your leadership work.

## TIME EACH DAY

However, to reiterate, leadership is not always an easy job to compartmentalize. The notion that you can get all of leadership done during scheduled time is very unlikely. Most of us in leadership roles know that you can't just be a leader when you have the time scheduled to do it. The role of an important leader often involves events and tasks that can't be put off. If there is a crisis on Monday, you can't say that Friday is my next administrative day so I will deal with the irate referring physician at the end of the week when it suits my schedule. Sometimes, in fact all too often, leadership challenges demand that other things wait. My experience with irate medical professionals and administrators is that right or wrong, their problems won't wait 4 days. The analogy here is like that in skiing. There is an old cliché that if you don't get wet you aren't really trying. In this case, if you are an important leader, you need to expect to be interrupted.

In fact, many leaders learn that the most memorable and high impact moments in their leadership role are often the unexpected events—the crisis, the surprise, the fire that needs to be put out. It isn't the carefully crafted report that they are remembered for, it is the time that they rolled up their sleeves during a crisis, took control and improvised a solution that worked. One of my administrative assistants once asked why I had a small, protected block of time that recurred on my calendar and then she laughed when I responded that it was for the future crises that would crop up. She thought that this was interesting so she kept track and it was remarkable how often it got used.

This really is the norm and not the exception for involved and important leaders. Despite your best efforts, those types of events can't always be pigeon holed and you may need to stop everything else to focus on a conflict or other critical issue. It is the nature of leadership that you need to be ready for anything. I was talking to former classmate who is now the mayor of a medium sized city and he put it very bluntly—everything that goes wrong is his problem so he has to respond and do it right away. Most of what he did that had a high impact was what wasn't on the schedule when he started that morning but instead came from dealing with what had come up unexpectedly.

## TIME FOR LEADERSHIP LEARNING

Allocating the time you need to lead should also include time for leadership training. This may include CME courses and symposia that focus on leadership, economics, and strategy. You may seek out more formal training through one of your professional organizations or even through an academic degree program. While you are already busy and you and your spouse and perhaps also your work colleagues may all resent you taking the time to do this, you have to set aside the time to work on becoming a better leader. It will turn out to be one of the best investments you can make. Whatever choices you do make, it is critical that you make the commitment to develop both your personal leadership skills and the core knowledge that together provide a foundation for enhancing your capabilities. Leaders need to be at the top of their game and since the challenges have never been greater than they are now that means committing yourself to constant improvement.

## TIME TO INTERACT WITH OTHER LEADERS: NETWORKING

Great leaders are usually very good at creating and maintaining a strong network of associations with other leaders, thinkers, and influencers in their fields. This gives them good streams of useful information, ideas and advice, helps them with forging relationships, and maintains access to sources of political and social power. This doesn't happen without work. It should be obvious, but it needs emphasizing that leaders need time to do this. At times, other (nonleading) members of a group of professionals may be highly critical of this type of work. They need to be educated that it is just part of the leader's job. They may be jealous of the leader who is spending time at a catered lunch while you are covering in a clinic, but they need to understand the importance of the leader and the value that his or her leadership networking brings to them and the group.

If the leader is doing this well, it is time very well spent. Activities like playing in a charity golf tournament with local celebrities may sound glamorous and may not seem like "work" compared to reading trauma computed tomography (CT) studies (unless you are a terrible golfer like me), but they are a necessary part of a leader's job and should be respected by the other members of the department or group. It sounds like a tautology or a Zen statement, but leaders need the time to do leadership tasks. Leaders need to lead and the only way that they can do it is if they have the resources that they need to succeed.

## KEY POINTS

1. Leaders need dedicated time to be able to lead well, in addition to their other responsibilities to their group or department.
2. Leaders require some flexibility in their schedules to do their job. Sometimes the most important things that they need to do are the unexpected issues that pop up.
3. Leadership requires time for training and maintenance. Just like being a good nurse or other type of professional, it takes work to become good and to stay good at what you do.
4. Leaders need to be good at relationships and networking in order to be successful in leading their group or department. Give yourself or them time to build networks that serve and protect your group.

*Image credit: © Frank Lexa*

# 15

# Leading Change in an Organization

*"Ch-ch-ch-ch-Changes, Turn and face the strange, Ch-ch-Changes"*
*—David Bowie, British artist, in "Change" song (1971), 1947–2016*

## INTRODUCTION

As we have discussed at other points in this book, one of the tasks of a leader is to help a group to change and adapt. This encompasses everything from big issues, such as crisis management to handling the more mundane challenges, such as taking on a new contract, managing personnel changes, or adopting new technologies. We have also covered leadership during crises in other chapters. In this section, we will turn to managing and leading in less dramatic, but in many cases much more important circumstances. For you as a leader, one of the things on your list of critical roles is to try to anticipate where your group will be in 5 years, that is, a topic we will cover in a future discussion. From your role as a strategic planner, you should be watching carefully for opportunities and threats on the horizon and then developing plans for handling them.

Change can come from many sources and you should be keeping an eye on multiple fronts including market, technologies, government, sociocultural landscape, new knowledge, novel scientific discoveries, and economic trends.

In this chapter, we are going to focus on your role of effective implementation of change and its management—how a leader helps his or her organization to adapt to changing circumstances. This forms the bridge from figuring where the group needs to go across to how to get the group or institution into the future effectively.

Leadership Lessons for Health Care Providers. http://dx.doi.org/10.1016/B978-0-12-801866-8.00015-9

# DYNAMICS IN UNDERSTANDING CHANGE

## Inevitability

The nature of change is problematic for many of us and in some ways particularly so for some healthcare professionals. As a leader, you need to both understand and communicate to your members that change is inevitable. This is easy to verbalize and many of us understand this at some level, but that doesn't prevent many, if not most of us, from being deeply resistant to acting on that knowledge. This is particularly true when the change is marked, when it disrupts our current ways of doing things and comes with costs. For many of us, there is a rather profound view that our careers will be relatively stable. At a minimum, we will get paid the same or more for our work, we will work about as hard, and we will have as much or more status as we do now. It is sobering to consider that over a 30–40 year career that will probably not be the case. Worse in some ways is that many professionals of my generation seemed until recently to have a very deep seated notion that the future will be kind to us, that is, that things will change, but only for the better. Unfortunately, many events in the early 21st century, both in and out of healthcare have suggested that at least in the short term, change can be very unkind. You as a leader need to anticipate both the positive and negative impact of change on your group and your institution.

An example may be helpful here in understanding why when healthcare workers think about change they sometimes focus only on the positive sides. I did some work with focus groups of physicians to understand the impact of a technology that was relatively new at the time—a picture archiving and communication system (PACS) that was part of the digital revolution in medical imaging. It replaced X-ray film images with digital files that could be seen and shared on computer systems. The physicians saw the positives—lower costs of film, easier archiving, faster results, and easier sharing of information, but most of them didn't immediately see or acknowledge the downsides—loss of face to face contact during consultations and the ease of outsourcing diagnostics to another state or country and disaggregating local relationships in a hospital or health system.

Many of us in healthcare instead prefer to believe in a future that will be a lot like the present or perhaps even more rosy without any jarring change associated with it. This lack of both realism and imagination blocks accurate assessment of both big threats and big opportunities to your organization. If the members of the organization understand that the institution needs to evolve in order to thrive, then change becomes easier to anticipate and to implement successfully to maximize the benefits and minimize the negatives of major change.

## Quality of Change: The Good, the Bad, and the Ugly

It should go without saying that not all change is good. Furthermore, it is worth emphasizing that some change is abjectly bad and much of the change that we see involves trade-offs. At some of the meetings I have been to in the healthcare sector, a "change management consultant" will tell the audience to "embrace change." Occasionally this is done to a thumping rock and roll soundtrack and once even included a light show as well to get the audience revved up about the excitement of embracing change in their hospital. We as healthcare professionals should be at least a step or two above this nonsense. Only someone with poorly controlled attention deficit/hyperactivity disorder would unthinkingly embrace change for change's sake. Separating changes into the good, the bad, and the ugly is part of your job as a leader. Decisions to make a change need to be analyzed in terms of costs, benefits, risks, rewards, etc. Mindlessly embarking on a wrenching transformation without thinking it through can be terrible for an institution and its loyal employees.

In your position as one of the leaders, you need to be cognizant and prepare for the downsides of change. Innovations like putting in voice recognition software or the use of tablets for data entry may have significant value, but they also carry negatives as well, particularly for the generation of professionals that is mid-career or later and now has to adapt to the change and give up some of their old habits and training.

## Change: Real and Imagined

Finally, not all that appears to be change is actually real. Sometimes leaders feel compelled to create the appearance of leadership without any serious consideration of whether or not there will be substantial change, let alone a positive effect. This rather childish idea of just doing something for the sake of image or of public relations, of "let's mix it up and see what happens" usually just creates the appearance or illusion of change rather than building new value and positive changes in the work environment. This is also often a prescription for conflict, friction, and waste and is unfortunately too common in our institutions. When you bring in outside consultants to a healthcare enterprise there may not be a detailed understanding of the culture of the medical world. There will also be a drive to show results for the money spent on the consultation. The combination can lead to overly quick implementation of change or changes without enough thought about the impact of the new direction that the consultants proposed.

Change for the sake of change rather than for substantive improvement can be both counterproductive and disruptive to a group. To put it even more bluntly, change is often stressful to your people and is hard to implement well. You as a leader should carefully consider whether your

plans for change will be worth it and only pursue those plans and directions that offer a genuine opportunity for positive changes that justify the
effort involved. Just creating motion without meaningful improvement
will hurt your organization and undermine your credibility as a leader. To
put it a bit more bluntly, most change, like most drugs (at least the ones
that work) has side effects. Like prescribing a drug, you need to weigh the
costs and benefits carefully.

# PROGRAMS FOR IMPLEMENTING
# IMPORTANT CHANGES

Another important aspect of your approach to change should be to
treat it as part of your overall strategy for management, rather than just
an occasional or worse episodic or ad hoc part of what you do. There are
many ways to develop a programmatic approach to handling change in a
systematic fashion.

## Kaizen: Gradual, Positive Change

One way to handle change is to have policies and practices in place that
craft your leadership approach to change as a core part of how you lead
and manage. In some institutions, this is deeply embedded in the structure
and organization of the organization. The idea of continuous, planned improvement was given the name Kaizen in Japan (see Imai, 1986).

For us in healthcare, this means rather than having a one time program
to do something like reduce waiting time in the Emergency Department, we
instead need to plan to do that continuously, every year improving that metric as well as other key measures of safety, quality, and performance. In this
environment, change is encouraged, measured, and managed continuously
rather than as a response to a crisis, an event (JACHO citation), or a whim of
a leader. If the notion of change becomes embedded in your culture and it is
handled well, then it is less traumatic for your team and can become a goal
for them in their careers rather than a burden to be overcome.

## Creative Destruction

A famous 20th century economist, Joseph Schumpeter, coined the term
"creative destruction" to describe one of the consequences of successful
innovation. In the realm of technology, the past several decades have seen
the typewriter, the eight track music deck and host of other technologies
marginalized and for the most part cast into the dustbin of history as was
the buggy whip a century ago with the rise of the automobile and of car
culture in developed nations. For you as a leader in healthcare, this means
being able to reevaluate technologies, services, and whole contracts on a

regular basis and ask the hard question of whether or not this is the time to let this go. Many leaders have trouble with this, because they or their friends may have made the decision to create these contracts or adopt those technologies. Implementing a technology and having your workforce go through training to use it creates a barrier to change.

One of the aspects of modern healthcare that puzzles some economists is why this doesn't happen more in healthcare. In my own profession of radiology, it is not uncommon for physicians to order multiple diagnostic tests or the wrong tests when only one is necessary. The new is added to the old rather than driving it out. This can result in unnecessary costs, unnecessary radiation exposure, and in some cases unnecessary medical adventures.

It helps to understand that in this case of creative destruction, change will free up resources for things that are better suited to the present day and to the future and that abandoning them early rather than later is the savvy decision. One of the better policies that some corporations and governments have in place are regular reviews and planning to abandon or sunset programs that are no longer effective. An insightful and helpful phrase that is adapted from some highly competitive industries that is useful to remember here is that your choice boils down to either making your old techniques and technologies obsolete yourself or facing obsolescence from competitors who do it better themselves.

## Planned Innovation

A last policy that you can implement as a leader is planned innovation. This is more far-sighted and thus more difficult to implement, particularly in challenging times like these. Nevertheless, it is a characteristic of highly successful individuals and organizations. This answers the question in the last section—do you want to be the innovator or the innovated. The English construction isn't the best, but you get the point—you want to be innovator who makes the decisions that leave others in the dust.

Change is one of the core challenges that really tests your mettle as a leader—can you balance preparing for the future with upsetting the status quo. Standing policies about continuous improvement, planned destruction, and abandonment for the greater good of the institution and a dedication to innovation will help embed these ideas and practices in the organization and help everyone prepare and adapt.

## SOME PRACTICAL ISSUES IN CHANGE EFFORTS

### Timing is Everything

As we discussed in the chapters on crisis leadership, those events can be catalysts for implementing change policies that should have been put in place anyway. If you are being threatened with a closure or loss of a contract, your institution will be much more amenable to making needed changes in order to survive. At the less extreme level, you should keep an eye open for windows of opportunity. It is easier to manage change when the circumstances are more propitious, but you need to balance waiting for a better time with the risks, benefits, and other factors that a delay would entail. Milestones, such as retirements, contract renewals, lease terminations, etc. should be anticipated and used to implement a change efficaciously.

## Start Small, Using Demonstration or Pilot Innovations

One of the best ways to implement a change in an institution of significant size is to start small. Instead of trying to change things at all six of your practice locations, try a pilot project at one. Demonstrate the value and work out the bugs before you do it across the entire organization. While some leaders prefer a fast, big, comprehensive roll out, the strategy of using a small demonstration project first is a time tested way to improving your chances of success when implementing a major change or novel program. This may seem obvious, but both my domestic and international work has shown that this tactic isn't used as often as it should be. There seem to be several reasons. First, is that once someone finally accepts that a change, a new plan, is necessary they want to get it over with. Like a flu shot or pulling off a bandage, they want it be as quick as possible. Instead, you are usually better off treating as a procedure made up of several steps rather than just one. Second, they often assume that there is enough information available right now to implement the plan. The insights from project management suggest that part of what happens when you implement change is that you learn, that is, some of the critical information comes in after the project starts, that is, it's not all there when you begin. Ponder that before your next project and you will probably have a higher likelihood of success.

## KEY POINTS

1. Change leadership is a core function of your leadership role. Learning to do it better will help you in many of the other tasks you face in your position.
2. Change and adapting to it is not optional, it is simply a fact in the modern work environment. Technology, political pressures, and societal changes all guarantee that your healthcare work will change during your career arc. Ignoring it in your job is no less critical than trying to ignore an oncoming truck in the wrong lane. You may not like it, you may be correct that the change is not even for the better, but ignoring it is neither a safe nor a sane option.
3. Change leadership and management will be easier for you and your organization if it is embedded in policies and smart practices rather done in an ad hoc fashion.

# INTERLUDE: MAKING THE PLUNGE—
# HOW TO BE A LEADER IN FOUR EASY STEPS

We are at roughly the half way mark and this is probably a good time to have a quick summary how to make the plunge and summarize some of the issues we have discussed to date, before we delve into some more difficult topics. I give lectures and talks at academic, scientific, and corporate meetings, and I try to close every talk with actionable points that the attendees can use when they get home. When I sit in on other speakers talks, I find it frustrating when after 30 or 45 min or more, there isn't actionable content. I may have been entertained but I really don't have anything from the talk to take home and use. Here we will review some summary steps in how to plunge into leadership on your own journey. Each is an actionable point that you should seriously consider (and occasionally reconsider) on your path to becoming a great leader.

## Ask Yourself if You Really Want to Be a Leader

One of the opening themes of this book is that almost everyone can be a leader. With the right motivation, the right training, and education, most of us can become good leaders. The deep question though is do you want this and do you want it for the right reasons. While not all of us will admit it, there is nothing wrong with wanting a leadership position because it will pay better or give you a better title, a better office, better parking, etc. Given the challenges they face and the value that they create, leaders (at least the good and great ones) deserve recognition and other rewards. However, you need to ask yourself better questions. Don't ask "do I want to have the benefits of being a leader," the answer should be pretty obvious. Everything else being equal, most of us would rather live in the White House and fly on Air Force one and be able to retire with gold plated benefits. Instead ask the smarter questions: do I want to lead? Can I put up with the challenges? Do I want to go into a new endeavor or will it be too much of a burden? Deep down would I rather just be a surgeon, a nurse, or a dentist and let someone else do the leadership work.

## If You Decide That You Want to Lead, You Aren't Done With the Introspection

I have been collaborating with Dr. David Fessel of the University of Michigan on a series of interviews with luminary leaders in my own field of diagnostic radiology. Our very first interviewee, Dr. James Thrall has been a luminary leader. He is a former chair of the American College of Radiology Board of Chancellors and retired chairman from both Henry Ford Hospital and the Massachusetts General Hospital.

Jim made many cogents points in his hour with us, one of which I will repeat here. He said that one of the keys to being a chairman is to be brutally introspective about not only your motivation as we discussed previously, but also about your strengths and weaknesses. This is not to say that if you find weaknesses you should give up your quest to be a leader. Far from it! There haven't been many faultless leaders in healthcare. But it means that you must know yourself and know that you can both handle your flaws and capitalize on your core capabilities.

## Throughout Your Career Cultivate Good Friends and Mentors

All of us need someone who can help us see where we are weak and where we need help. Sometimes when you are a candidate for an academic promotion or a leadership position they may ask for over a dozen recommendations as part of your application. While you may be caught up in the competitive aspects of this—a race to be won, a competition to beat the other candidates, you may be missing the more important question.

Before you throw your hat into the ring, you should probably grab three or maybe even a dozen of your trusted mentors and advisors and ask them their opinions. Ask them to be honest, to be candid, even brutally so about the job and your qualifications. A good friend will help provide perspectives on what you have overlooked. She or he will tell you what you need to fix, that is, change the list of responsibilities, get a vice chair to cover a part of the department's activity where you are weak—in order to improve your chances of success. Also, she or he may say that yes you should be a unit supervisor, but not this year or not in this place. This may sound burdensome to some readers, but if you can't take criticism and challenging advice from your trusted friends, you may find that your career path will be a stormy one.

## Make a Commitment

By now you may be tired of reading this, but no leader is perfect. You may have doubts about yourself, but if you and your friends agree that you will be a good leader then go for it. The medical world needs good leaders and it certainly needs better leaders. I have worked in my share of places over the years and I have never met a perfect leader. Moreover, the best ones know that they are imperfect and they handle that in their own way. The ones who think that they are perfect are often the ones who are the hardest to work with—they can't see their own flaws (but may have an eidetic–photographic-memory for the mistakes and weaknesses of those around them). You can do better (and you will) than many of the people who came before you.

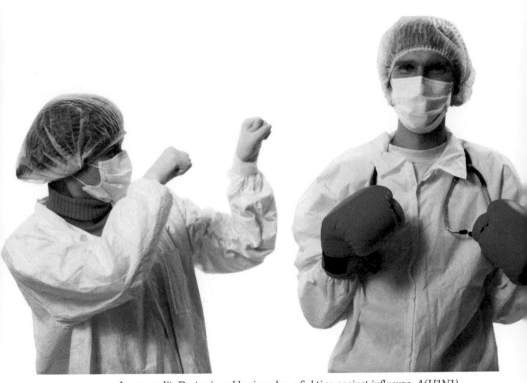

*Image credit: Doctor in red boxing gloves fighting against influenza, A(H1N1).*
*© aptyp_koK/Shutterstock*

# 16

# Leadership in Conflict

*"Illegitimi non carborundum"*
*—as used by the Harvard Marching Band*

## INTRODUCTION

In an article, I once discussed the importance of adhering to principles and maintaining ethics in your role as a leader (Lexa, 2010b). Sometimes when I discuss this in a lecture, people think that this means that you should be soft, just try to please everyone you interact with in your work, and don't make waves. That was not and certainly isn't what I think about leadership. However if you think that yourself, you wouldn't be alone if you did. Many leaders in science and medicine do shy away from inter-personal conflict, hoping that rationality and good will are all that it will take them to lead well. Unfortunately in the rough and tumble world we live in, you also have to be willing to be tough and at times quite hard if you are going to be an effective leader. This doesn't mean that you have to give up your principles. Ethics aren't only for the peaceful times—in fact if you really want to understand someone's true character, it is usually the tough times and the testing that comes with it that will determine what they are really made of. You can be fair and ethical, but still be tough as nails when the situation warrants.

In fact, the real test of your principles and perhaps your ethics and morals, is how you handle the pressure of the tough choices. As times become more challenging and enemies arise, it is likely that you will have to handle more conflict than you have had in the past. Even in the midst of a battle there are still right and wrong ways of handling a tough conflict. This column will discuss some of the more unpleasant truths of leadership and how to handle them.

# SEPARATE EMOTIONS FROM PEOPLE
# AND SITUATIONS

Getting angry or upset in a difficult situation isn't going to help you. It may seem like a normal response and some leaders do respond quickly with yelling, cursing, slamming doors, etc. In fact, in many situations, this will be a serious detriment to your leadership. In many nations, an inability to control yourself during conflict will be seen as a loss of face. This can be a fatal flaw in some cultures, a sign that you are not up to the task. The perception is that if you can't control yourself, then how can you control others, let alone guide an organization or institution. The converse is often very unsettling to your opponents—if you can remain cool, calm, and focused while they are out of control, it is very unnerving. They are expecting you to drop to their level. If you can rise above, you are in a much better position to manage yourself, to hold your team together, and to come up with smart strategies and tactics. Anger and fear will cloud your judgement.

In traditional business schools, students are often put together in small learning teams of five or so people for most of their first year courses. This forces them to work with people who are often very different from themselves. They come from all walks of life, from varying job and cultural backgrounds, have different ethical standards and varying commitment and dedication to their work. Being on a learning team, where your work and your grades will depend on those people, forces you to learn to manage both your team and yourself. This is a particular challenge when you can't choose them and you are forced to play the hand that you are dealt. You need to learn to effectively handle your emotions as well as theirs. Great leaders still have feelings, but they learn to see the strategic possibilities and separate the people from the issues. They don't let those feelings (both positive and negative) cloud their judgment.

When you face someone in a difficult situation, you can't let your anger make you stupid. It is normal to get angry in these situations, but strong leaders learn to figure out how to stay calm and how to win in the situation anyway. I have personally been involved in team versus team negotiations where we had to pull someone from the team because they had become so enraged that they were cursing and practically foaming at the mouth. That level of anger and the loss of control was too disruptive and was bringing out bad behavior on both sides. The team members who weren't involved in the fighting were becoming demoralized. The negotiations were in danger of breaking down completely so we had to intervene. As the leader, you have to stay in control of yourself if you are to perform at your best and also be able to help your team to perform at its best.

A very interesting phenomena that you see in some business and law situations is faux anger—the businessperson on the team who deliberately acts the role of the "bad cop," makes angry statements, and then storms out of the room. Then the remaining members of the team act as good cops to try to pull the negotiation together. An example of this from history is that of Nixon and Kissinger. When Richard Nixon was President and Henry Kissinger was the Secretary of State they would often play good cop/bad cop. Not surprising perhaps for those of us who lived through that period, Nixon was the bad actor. He would make threats and angry statements. Kissinger would then point out that if the person on the other side of the table didn't make concessions in the negotiation then Kissinger would not be able to control what that crazy guy Nixon would do. In their recollections to journalists, they saw this as a fairly effective approach to tough negotiation. In other areas of life, this is a tactic that some people use (and overuse), but understand that you need to be in control of yourself and your team when you are in a tough conflict situation and if you do act crazy or angry, make sure that it is just an act.

## WORK FROM PRINCIPLES

Another one of the more unpleasant tasks for leaders is delivering bad news. Despite all the talk in recent years about 360 degree feedback in the work place and the current enthusiasm for regular performance reviews, reprimanding a coworker is still a necessary leadership task. This is one of the unpleasant aspects of leadership and many leaders shy away from delivering bad news. Given the performance pressure in many healthcare organizations today, setting expectations and delivering both praise and criticism is a task that leaders have to be willing to take on themselves in some situations and perhaps delegate in other.

Worse, the even more stressful task of having to fire a peer appears to be becoming more common now in some medical groups than in the past (L. Muroff, in personal communication). This is particularly painful in groups of professionals where everyone knows each other and considers their coworkers both colleagues and friends. Many private medical groups and organizations are the opposite of the stereotype of the large, faceless corporation. Unless the group is very large and/or is widespread geographically, most people do know each other, see each other as peers, and usually want to be friendly and collegial. In many groups, people develop relationships with each other outside of work. They may go to events outside of work together, their kids are friends, they go to the same religious and social organizations together, etc. That close knit nature makes these types of decisions particularly challenging and disruptive.

In a difficult situation like this, it is imperative that the actions you take be based upon principles and norms of behavior. You need to demonstrate consistency and integrity in how you handle a difficult case. Did you punish the last person the same way? Are you playing favorites or are you clear and fair? These are also not just issues of how your leadership is perceived, they also have legal ramifications that you need to clearly understand before you act. This book is not intended to substitute for legal advice. As a leader, you need to know when you need expert advice and this is one of those domains where you need a smart HR policy and a smart legal advisor.

## STARTING TROUBLE IS USUALLY A SYMPTOM OF WEAKNESS

A well-worn cliché about office politics is only start fights that you can win. That may not be true for great leadership. In your career, you may need to take on conflicts that put your career and your group at risk. Being a coward may hurt you as much as being a troublemaker. However, always be careful and think it through carefully before you initiate a conflict. Most experienced leaders will tell you that looking for trouble is a fool's errand. No matter how much they may itch for a fight and enjoy the adrenaline rush of entering a conflict, they know that great leaders choose their fights carefully. Another old cliché, this one about the American Presidency, is that the President doesn't need to look for trouble. Most of them are not in power long before trouble finds them. Recent history certainly supports this notion. In my lifetime, every president has faced unexpected crises and moreover many administrations have been defined by exactly those untoward events and how they were handled rather than by the vision the president had going into the office. A recent example is that the 43rd president, George W. Bush, had run on a platform and expected to lead on a program of domestic and economic reforms. Instead, on Sep. 11, 2001, he became a wartime president and will be remembered predominately for those acts rather than the domestic agenda that he originally envisioned.

In closing, understand that conflict is part of the landscape that you will face as a leader. If you handle it in a principled, smart fashion then you will succeed here as in the other tasks that you face. As the opening quote points out, don't make trouble and enemies unless you intend to do so and can live with the consequences. Not initiating conflict is usually a good strategy, but since conflict is often inevitable you need to be ready and to lead through it. In a future column we will discuss how to handle situations where your side contemplates starting a battle.

## KEY POINTS

1. Separate people from issues
2. Separate your emotions from the task at hand
3. Manage yourself first—if the leader loses control your group is in trouble
4. Keep to your strategy and be true to your principles. Conflicts shouldn't be the exception to how you behave in your work life—in fact they are acid tests of who you really are.

*Image credit: Photo of a damaged building taken by Bert Cohen after the 1948 Fukui Earthquake; Wikimedia Commons*

# 17

# Leading in a Crisis

*"A leader is best when people barely know he exists, when his work is done, his aim fulfilled, they will say: we did it ourselves"*
**—Lao Tzu, ancient Chinese philosopher and founder of Taoism**

## INTRODUCTION

There is a misperception that has been around for decades that the Mandarin character for crisis contains elements that mean both danger and opportunity. While incorrect, this meme persists, partly through poor scholarship, but also because the idea is so compelling. The notion that crises contain opportunity is an optimistic idea and perhaps even something of a heroic ideal. That said, many of the crises that you will face will likely seem to you to contain more danger than opportunity. As a leader, don't ignore the chance to find the good in a crisis.

Crises, whether mild or severe, whether more dangerous or not, are the times that truly test our leaders. For those of us in medicine in the United States, few would argue with the observation that we are in the midst of a crisis that is real, is severe, and has truly dangerous elements. For many of us, our reimbursement has been cut hard and will likely be cut again by not only the next government but probably those that follow. The notion that healthcare reform was a one time event that occurred in Mar. of 2010 will prove naïve and it is likely that it will be an issue for not only our generation but also for the ones that follow. Crises in healthcare have also arisen from other directions. Traditional boundaries of professional domains have been challenged by turf wars as well as by new entrants into the field of healthcare delivery. Many types of professionals have been challenged in the turf from below, from peers, from above, and from those the traditional domain of healthcare professionals. That is a lot of challenges.

More broadly, costs, access, and quality continue to present challenges and pressures to change healthcare in both the public and private sectors. In my field, denial of studies in radiology benefit management companies has also grown significantly and now affects the care of 75 million

Leadership Lessons for Health Care Providers. http://dx.doi.org/10.1016/B978-0-12-801866-8.00017-2

Americans (see Iglehart, 2009). Other forms of rationing and revenue reduction measures are likely as the healthcare overhaul which began in 2010 progresses through its next phases.

In some sectors, we are not training enough health professionals domestically to handle either the aggregate growth in work or the changing nature of our workflow due to factors of call, specialization, higher levels of complexity and intensity of care, etc. These challenges combine to create crises but it should be clear to you that this is the time for great leadership and in this chapter we will begin our first instalment in discussing how leaders should react in a crisis.

## PREVENTION TRUMPS REACTION

"Do the difficult things while they are easy and do the great things while they are small"

*—Lao Tzu*

The first step to becoming a great leader in a crisis is paradoxically not to have to lead in a crisis. This may sound like misprint or a Zen statement but ponder it before you reject it. While no leader is immune from surprises, the best leaders aggressively anticipate and manage in order to prevent crises or at least contain issues in advance rather than merely reacting to them once they have truly grown to critical proportions. To put it a bit differently, a savvy leader aims to prevent most fires from starting in the first place or at least handles them before they are out of control as the 2500-year-old quote from Lao Tzu states elegantly. Leaders who are adept at this type of strategic planning are usually also well positioned to deal with the crises that they cannot anticipate nor prevent.

At the other extreme, the weakest leaders, including some of the narcissists we described in an earlier chapter (Levels II), actually welcome crises or in the extreme case even create them. They do this in order to be the hero who intervenes to save the day and take the glory. This can lead to some of the most terrible forms of destructive management in which only the leader benefits but looks good to those people too foolish to see and understand what has really happened.

## CRISIS MANAGEMENT: PHASES

Analyzing the role of smart guidance in a crisis is facilitated by understanding that smart leadership involves several phases of tasks and thinking. We can demystify and better understand good leadership by breaking it down into those phases and tasks that provide a framework for crisis management.

## Step 1: Preparation

First, there is the preparation phase. This includes what we have discussed previously in the strategic planning phase. It may also include running drills for known types of crises, such as mass casualty, real fires, etc. It may include setting aside reserves or cutting costs before a revenue crunch hits. It also encompasses all the elements of smart management that a good leader should establish in good times. That foundation leaves you better prepared when storms hit. It also establishes relationships and trust within your group that will serve you well when the organization is stressed.

One test of great leadership is asking the question of "what if." Does your leader have an answer to questions like: What will happen if the government cuts our reimbursement by 15%? What will happen if our payments from the hospital become bundled under a global payment scheme? What can we do if the hospital administrator threatens not to renew our contract? What if we can't hire another important specialist in our group by Jul. 1? What if the nursing staff is cut by 10%? A great leader and a great organization consider these questions in advance and make contingency plans for such events. One of the striking traits of successful leaders in the corporate, political, and military worlds is how much time they devote to thinking about these issues. They are rarely caught unawares by current events and have plans in place to deal with them. Lesser leaders act surprised when events hit and then scramble to catch up and react. In healthcare, a smart group and a smart leader will have contingency plans for the types of crises that are reasonably foreseeable, such as those mentioned previously. This is not to say that you need to spend time developing a plan for an asteroid hitting the Earth—that is probably not going to be something that you address directly within your dermatology practice. Instead focus on things that meet a combination of several criteria: likelihood of occurrence, likelihood of impact on your group in healthcare, and where planning can help to ameliorate impact and improve outcomes through planning, management, and effective leadership.

## Step 2: Execution

"Plans are nothing, planning is everything"
—*Dwight D. Eisenhower, 34th President of the USA, 1890–1869*

The second of the three stages, is when the actual crisis begins. Your department receives notice of a freeze on hiring from the dean, but your clinical work is on the rise due to an influx of new patients. How do you prepare your faculty to handle the implications of this for their clinical workloads, their academic time, etc.? Do you have a plan for how to redistribute clinical commitments while maintaining the academic missions of your department.

In crisis management, begin with what you already know. If you have a business plan or better yet have discussed your contingencies and options with your group then this is the moment of truth. Even if your contingency plans aren't directly on point for how the crisis unfolds, you are well prepared to think clearly, avoid panic, and execute your responses in real time. You can ask the right questions, get the right information, and make the right moves faster than you would be able to do if you had not done your preparation. As the quote from former General Eisenhower, a truly great military planner, points out, the process of planning is more important than the details of a plan.

The next step is to put together a core group within your organization who can carry out your plans and keep up with the flow of information in a crisis. While you would hope that the whole group would act professionally and show good citizenship, that is not always the case. Having a trusted inner circle will help you to pull through the difficult times while moving fast and staying smart. As we have discussed at other points, it is also critical to distribute leadership and you will need help at this stage.

At this point, you also need to make sure that you disseminate information quickly and accurately to the entire organization that you lead. One of the most common misconceptions that leaders have is that they should hold back bad news. Many people honestly believe in the "mushroom" hypothesis of professional communication—keep your underlings in the dark and feed them manure (or sometimes repeated using other less polite terms). That is a poor way to treat smart professionals. They will worry and they won't be able to help you unless they have the correct information. Rumors and misinformation will spread quickly unless you take the initiative to pass along accurate, critical data quickly and share your decisions as soon as appropriate. While you don't need to share everything, not giving out important information during a crisis is generally a poor leadership decision for professional organizations. If you stonewall your staff or worse if you lie to hide bad news from professionals or because you have made stupid decisions, your ability to lead will crumble quickly.

At a personal level, it is important that you be engaged with your organization and be personally involved in the crisis. The leader who tells the membership to tighten their belts and work harder while simultaneously helping themselves to a bonus is not just a hypocrite, they are incompetent leaders and should be fired. A leader who genuinely shares the pain of hers or his team is not only better at leading because he or she is at the leading edge, they are also more motivated to truly address a crisis than someone with little or no skin in the game. If the hospital announces that the nurses and/or physicians will need to take on extra clinical duties, does the leadership roll up their sleeves and do their share or do they give orders and then leave to go to the golf course?

Another piece of time tested advice is that during the crisis, you need to pay much closer attention to your decisions and the outcomes. Your attention to detail within the inner circle needs to ratchet up so that you can react quickly to changing events. This phase is so important that we will revisit it elsewhere in this book.

## Step 3: Recovery and Analysis

You might think that once a crisis has abated your role in crisis management is over. For many of us the time crunch, the emotional exhaustion, and the other stresses of the crisis make us want to immediately get back to normalcy and forget the crisis as soon as it is over. However, leaders who have to deal with life and death crises routinely in their careers are either trained to understand or eventually figure out that their work isn't over when the crisis ends. They know that they should do postcrisis analyses to understand what happened, examine what was done correctly, and figure out what to do to prepare for the next crisis. These are known by several names including "after action analyses." Smart organizations learn from crises in large part because their leader knows that crises will happen again. Sensible leaders know that this won't be the last time that budgets are threatened or that governments change any more than reasonable people who live in certain parts of the world would expect to have seen their last earthquake or hurricane. They are smart enough to know that there will be another and another one after that. While the specific time and intensity may not be predictable, the fact is that these things will recur and you had better be ready.

A great leader sits down afterward to mull over what they did right and what went wrong. No team performs perfectly, particularly in the heat of a crisis. Some of your individuals will shine and some will show less desirable aspects of their true characteristics in the midst of the stress. One of the reasons for great preparation is knowing that performance is degraded by fear, confusion, and other factors in times of crisis. Involve your inner circle to perform an "after action" analysis to examine how things went. Listen to everyone and get multiple perspectives on how well your team reacted. The rationale for this is two fold: (1) first is to understand how your preparation and execution worked and how you can do better the next time; (2) the second reason is that this is the time that the leader needs to rethink who on their staff is leadership material and who didn't pass muster. The crisis tested all of you and this is the time that you need to reevaluate your staffing in time to prepare for the next crisis.

## KEY POINTS

1. Great leadership in a crisis begins with anticipating and preventing crises from occurring. Great planning and strategic thinking is a hallmark of successful leaders.
2. Crises have phases, each with distinct opportunities for successful leadership.
3. Leadership doesn't end when the crisis abates or resolves. Great leaders learn from high stress situations and use them to prepare for future challenges.

*Image credit: The Crystal Ball Artist, by John William Waterhouse, ca. 1902; Wikimedia Commons*

# 18

# Tough Choices: How Leaders Make the Hard Decisions

## INTRODUCTION

Leaders face decisions big and small. Some fall into the very easy category—when to hold a meeting, what color should the new carpeting be, etc. They don't warrant much time or effort. The middle level of decisions are covered elsewhere in this book. In this chapter, we want to talk about one of the serious downsides of leadership—the tough, hard decisions. The ones that don't have a good outcome, that are emotionally draining, the ones that involve hard choices and leave some parties (or perhaps everyone) feeling bad. There aren't easy answers to these questions and there aren't easy answers to how to make them. The opening graphic at the beginning of this chapter is meant to be humorous, but in real life I have known more than leader who will admit (at least in private) to using a coin flip to decide who to fire in a tough situation.

## WHAT ARE THE HARD DECISIONS?

Difficult decisions come in many forms. For medical leaders, some of the characteristics of the tough ones are as follows:

Novelty—I've never done this before
Emotional—I am personally involved and the emotions—anger, loss, envy, concern, etc. make it hard
Ambiguity—I don't have enough information to make the decision and I don't know how to get it
Responsibility without authority—I don't really have the power I need to do the right thing

Leadership Lessons for Health Care Providers. http://dx.doi.org/10.1016/B978-0-12-801866-8.00018-4

Wicked problems—there isn't an easy answer or a right answer. All the decisions have significant trade-offs and there may not be any certainty about the long-term outcome (for further details see Jha and Lexa, 2014)

Factions—there is no solution that will make everyone happy and you need to take a side

## DEALING WITH DIFFICULT DECISIONS

There are several things that good leaders do to handle difficult decisions and we will handle them in temporal order from prevention, through execution, and then follow up. Doing these things won't alleviate your exposure to difficult decisions, but they will prepare you for them and help minimize the damage to your group and to you as a leader when they do happen. As we have discussed elsewhere in this book these are the situations that often define us in ways that the more mundane business of leadership does not.

### Preparation and Prevention

Great leaders work at not being surprised. It still happens and you will encounter examples of that in this book. To help with your leadership performance in your career, let's discuss how you can prepare for (and either ameliorate or perhaps even prevent the need for) a difficult decision.

Anticipation of issues is a hallmark of great leadership. As we will note in a later chapter, Sun Tzu wrote in the Art of War, battles are won or lost before they are fought. Great leaders can head off hard decisions by expecting them and preparing for them. When difficult decisions need to be made, having anticipating a situation—hospital merger, forced consolidation, the sudden departure of an important member of your group, etc., the prepared leader is the one who can handle the situation and the decisions that it requires. They are the ones who don't panic and even sometimes make it easy.

### The Process of a Hard Decision

If you have ever worked with a leader as she or he works on a tough decision, there are several things that distinguish the effective leader from the mediocre and from the problem leader. The first is calm under fire. Leaders need to project outward calm. If they panic then that will inflame the situation and make it harder.

Second, they need to listen to more than one viewpoint. Hard decisions usually include elements of risk, complexity and multiple viewpoints can help in managing those high stakes issues. Third, they need to communicate effectively. If you are making a tough decision such as downsizing a clinical service then you need to spend a lot of time explaining how this will affect patient care, the practitioner's jobs, quality and safety, etc. Lots of people may be affected and communication and effective explanation are necessary. Lack of it can make the decision and its execution much more difficult.

## Execution and Followup

As you bring the decision forward and implement it, use a team. Try to have as many sides and stakeholders involved. Your job isn't to make everyone happy (nice though if you can) but instead to do the right thing for the group, the department, or institution that is affected. Pay close attention and followup. That will do several things including: (1) helping you avoid having a new hard decision if you don't do this one correctly through to resolution (2) helping you to learn from hard decisions. This one won't be your last.

### KEY POINTS

1. Anticipate hard decisions. Important leaders need to be ready for them.
2. Don't shy away from hard decisions but also don't underestimate them. Some are not only hard, they are wicked.
3. As the cliché goes, when faced with a hard decision, keep calm and (try) to carry on.
4. Use a process for handling the difficult decisions. A template or checklist will help you avoid errors and make the difficult things a bit easier.

*Image credit: President Kennedy addresses the 2506 Cuban Invasion Brigade, 29 December 1962, by Cecil W. Stoughton*

# 19

# Leadership and Mistakes

*A great nation is like a great man:*
*When he makes a mistake, he realizes it.*
*Having realized it, he admits it.*
*Having admitted it, he corrects it.*
*He considers those who point out his faults as his most benevolent teachers.*
*He thinks of his enemy as the shadow he himself casts.*
**—Tao Te Ching, Chinese classic text attributed to Lao Tzu**

## INTRODUCTION

One of the hardest things to handle in the medical field is a clinical mistake that affects a patient. This is particularly tough in my field of diagnostic radiology. We leave permanent records both of our images and our reports, so that if we miss a finding or misinterpret a finding on a diagnostic imaging examination like a CT or an MRI, those mistakes are usually available forever. Missing an important finding, such as the presence of intracranial blood or a cervical spine fracture will often have severe consequences for everyone involved: most of all for our patients and their families, but also for our referring clinical colleagues, our institutions, and for ourselves. The combination of a permanent recording as well as easy digital distribution means that our professional peers can easily find our errors in the system. This aspect of medical work drives a fear of failure and a consequent drive for perfectionism in clinical endeavors by all types of medical professionals. That is all well and good in the clinical arena, but it can be quite problematic in some other areas, such as the realm of leadership. Perfectionism and fear of failure can limit you as leader. Indecision and paralysis while waiting for more information or better opportunities is not always an option. With regard to danger, the safest road is not always the right one on your leadership path. Sometimes risks need to be taken and sometimes ambiguity needs to be tolerated if it can't be eliminated. In this chapter, we will explore

Leadership Lessons for Health Care Providers. http://dx.doi.org/10.1016/B978-0-12-801866-8.00019-6

the nature of imperfect leaders and how you can learn to be a better (though never perfect) leader.

## ILLUSIONS OF PERFECTIONISM

I also happen to be a private pilot and will borrow an important concept that I learned during that period of my life. When you enter into flight training with an aviation instructor, one of her/his tasks is to evaluate your personality. Several personality traits and "adverse mental states" are considered by experienced aviation professionals as red flags for high risk in the aeronautical environment. Not everyone who wants to become a pilot should be one. An important personality trait that is emphasized in training and also in the literature is a sense of invulnerability. Stated simply, people who think that they are perfect are dangerous. The trainees who don't believe that they can get lost in the night, who would never run out of gas, or couldn't possibly miss something important on a checklist are at higher risk for making mistakes than people who have a more realistic sense of the potential dangers of flight. Those dangers require training, preparation, and appropriate caution. If you believe that you can't make a mistake, that you are invulnerable, then you are not the right person to work in that dangerous, demanding environment because you won't take the time and effort to make sure that you are doing the right thing to stay in the air safely. Instructors need to assess if this is something that can be rectified or if you just aren't the kind of person who should be at the controls of an airplane by yourself. This issue is also true for the role of a leader. If you are blind to the fact that you are not perfect you will be resistant both to advice from other and to taking action yourself that could make you better in leadership tasks. If you think that getting tenure or a promotion to an high level position with an important title and a corner office makes you omniscient or perfect, you have just become a liability both to yourself and also to the people around you. Leaders who feel invulnerable are putting their organizations at risk by not being able to avoid and/or recover properly from mistakes.

Do any of you know a perfect physician, nurse, dentist, or other professional? You may know many great ones, but of course you haven't met someone who is perfect. The problem isn't the lack of perfection. Instead it is a combination of how good you really are and how self-aware you are. Are you blind to your failings? Do you catch your mistakes? Do you listen when someone else tells you about a problem that you missed or do you go into denial mode, both to the messenger and yourself? Having a big blind spot, compounds your human frailty and makes you more vulnerable.

All of us, however, have the capacity to be better at the things we do and that includes leadership. While leaders should know better, the fallacy of invulnerability is sometimes paradoxically worse in people who have become leaders. At a lower level in the organization, your lack of selfawareness might not matter so much or the decisions you make may not be as important. Leaders however have additional issues that arise from their positions and responsibilities (and often personalities) that can amplify their risk exposure to the invulnerability flaw. The reasons for this are fascinating and are discussed at length in a book by Carol Tavris and Elliot Aronson: *Mistakes Were Made (But Not by Me): Why We Justify Foolish Beliefs, Bad Decisions, and Hurtful Acts.*

As we have said elsewhere, leadership is murkier than many of the things that we do in the medical field. It has more variables and a larger matrix of choices than trying to decide whether or not there is a loss of gray–white differentiation on an ER head CT. Yet even in the latter case, my colleagues and I have all seen smart radiologists try to squirm their way out of a miss. The same holds true for a decision to transfer a patient, extract a tooth, or do a knee replacement. Rather than admit a mistake, we try to deny or perhaps self-justify the mistake. The smarter physician or leader follows the aforementioned advice of Lao Tzu and admits and learns from their mistakes so that they are better prepared for the next case. While we will never be perfect, we can be better at what we do and we can be better at handling our imperfection.

## THE LOOKING GLASS

In their book, Tavris and Aronson give a wide range of examples, from politics and science and corporate worlds, all the way to the clergy of terrible mistakes that leaders have made but then refuse to admit and handle in a clear and appropriate fashion. The authors make the point that this is not the same as an outright lie to the public. While deliberate lying is wrong in its own right, self-justification is also a form of lying to yourself and others. This may be more subtle than baldly lying, but it is quite dangerous both to yourself and to others. Even when errors are clear (wars that go badly, children are molested by trusted adults, deficits spin out of control, websites have disastrous launches, etc.), the leaders who are supposed to be responsible and in charge may limit the discussion by only acknowledging the obvious facts that the public already knows. They then try to escape personal responsibility by using a passive voice as in the title of the aforementioned book. In the very complicated world we live in this strategy does sometimes work. A likeable public figure sometimes succeeds in distancing themselves from a mess that they created. The more interesting question is who is getting fooled and why.

One of the most interesting aspects of this is that self-justification is a way of relieving the cognitive dissonance in the leader that would otherwise occur. Too few leaders have the courage to admit their personal mistakes caused the problem. This would require admitting that they are imperfect and many leaders seem to think that perfection is either a job requirement or was somehow conferred from on high when they got the job. Since these people are usually smart enough to understand that something went wrong, they often develop elaborate rationales for their mistakes that either deny reality or push the blame onto "others." It is the fault of another department, of "those guys or gals." This acknowledgement without really taking responsibility seems to be rampant in the standard media declarations that are made after major screw ups in the corporate and political fields.

One of the keys to great leadership that we have discussed elsewhere in this book is the need to first manage yourself. This is a hard task which shouldn't be underestimated and this chapter focuses on one of the hardest elements—can you be the great leader that Lao Tzu describes by overcoming this blind spot problem? If you aren't willing to take an honest look, then you will not learn from your mistakes, let alone learn to prevent them.

Another problem is that many leaders refuse to admit their errors, at least in public, because of the fear that they will lose their positions. This is not unfounded—they may well lose status or their leadership role. Depending on the role, the culture and their history, they may well be fired for serious mistake. Therefore they hope that by ignoring their mistakes they will go unnoticed or be forgotten. Shining light on them may amplify the publicity and increase their personal career risk. However, hiding leadership mistakes rarely works out in the long run. To use an analogy that we have encountered elsewhere in this work, the only US president to resign, Richard Nixon, was threatened with impeachment not for the burglary that occurred during his administration, but rather for the elaborate cover up and related crimes that ensued in what became known as the Watergate scandal.

If you think that you are immune to this, ask yourself how hard you have inventoried your own decisions. How many of you have counted up the number of bad decisions that you made on the job in the past year? To take it to a personal level, how many of us would frankly admit that we voted for the wrong person? How about admitting that you sent your child to the wrong school for 4 years (or twelve)? Most of us do the opposite, we look for reinforcing data to provide post hoc support for our decisions. We end up owning our decisions, both the good and bad without taking a hard enough look at the latter and instead looking for rationales for why they really weren't bad decisions. The better you can objectively analyze your decisions, the better you will be able to learn from them and do better the next time.

## KEY POINTS

1. Strive for perfection, but know that it is impossible. The greatest leaders are still human and make mistakes.
2. Know your blind spots, all of us have them. Try to reduce yours.
3. Find people who can tell you truth about your management decisions. You need people who can give you advice and even criticism. This requires a high level of trust and is never easy medicine to take, but it is worth it.
4. A small mistake is still a mistake. Ask yourself if you have gone down the wrong road. Paying attention to your errors and being honest about them with yourself (and where appropriate others as well) can prevent small mistakes from compounding into crises.
5. When you do make a mistake be willing to acknowledge it. Be willing to learn from it, to correct it, and to move on. You don't need to dwell on it, just fix it and get on with your work.

# The New York Times

LATE CITY EDITION
Weather: Partly sunny today; cool tonight. Partly sunny tomorrow. Temp. range: today 64-70; Friday 66-64. Highest Temp.-Hum. Index yesterday: 73. Details on Page 46.

VOL.CXXIII...No.42,567

NEW YORK, SATURDAY, AUGUST 10, 1974

15 CENTS

# FORD SWORN IN AS PRESIDENT; ASSERTS 'NIGHTMARE IS OVER'
## Nixon Bids an Emotional Farewell to Washington

### TEARS AT PARTING

#### Ex-President Warns Against Bitterness and Revenge

By JAMES T. WOOTEN

Gerald R. Ford takes the Presidential oath, administered by Chief Justice Warren E. Burger. Mrs. Ford attends. the White House ceremony.

### A Plea to Bind Up Watergate Wounds

By MARJORIE HUNTER

**G.M. to Raise Prices 9.5%**
On 1975 Cars and Trucks

**PAPERS AND TAPES** Aide Doubtful That Ford
Would Give Nixon Pardon

# 20

# Thinking About Failures in Leadership

*Bones heal, chicks dig scars, pain is temporary, glory is forever*
*—Evel Knievel, American legendary motorcycle daredevil, 1938–2007*

## INTRODUCTION

As we have discussed, most of the health professionals that you and I know are probably perfectionists or at least have strong tendencies in that direction. This is not a criticism and in fact it is critically important in clinical professions like ours. Most of us are involved in life and death decisions on a daily basis. You want your nurse, your dentist, and your surgeon to try their hardest to get every decision. We are trained this way and we try to practice this way so it is no surprise that we should want to get it right on every patient, every time. We have trained long and hard to get to the point where we are the experts, the ones who can provide superior care in difficult cases. The consequences for failure are high and our culture can be very tough on those who err. All of us probably know a health professional (or two or more…) who has a photographic memory for mistakes and can recall events in your department from 20 years ago.

However, that desire to always be right, to know it all and to never make nor tolerate a mistake can also limit our effectiveness when we branch out into other endeavors. This seems to be one of the reasons that physicians and some other health professionals are often reluctant to do things, such as take on leadership roles, to do practice building work, to participate in marketing, etc. Those areas lie in foreign territory that is far away from the comfort zones that you have mastered, such as the differential diagnosis of cerebello pontine angle lesions to the treatment of patients with complex immune mediated disease.

When health professionals do take on leadership roles, they are often distressed by the fact that leadership, particularly the best kinds of leadership, will involve at least some failure. The reasons are legion, including incomplete information, time pressures, and conflicting goals among many others. It may sound paradoxical, but only the most cautious, most cowardly leaders get through their tenure at the top without having made mistakes, both big and small. The paradox here is that those types of ineffective leaders usually do even more damage to the institutions that they serve.

## JUDGING "FAILURES"

Great leadership will involve meeting crises head on, trying to innovate, and taking risks, all of which will likely lead to both wins and losses in the short term. The complaining by colleagues tends to focus on the short term and on the setbacks. Furthermore, for the great leaders, those stumbles and failures are often the stuff of "water cooler" discussions by colleagues. Most of us have had that experience of listening to a partner complain about the latest project from the top and then carping about it and its limitations.

I am often asked at the top medical meetings about my views on other leaders in my profession. I refuse to accept the snap judgment that the other person is either offering and/or trying to elicit from me. There are many reasons for why I am reluctant to critique others, but three are foremost. First, unless you really understand the specifics of a person's situation it is impossible to accurately judge whether they made the right decision in a tough situation. Hearing about a situation second hand is simply too limited to evaluate it. You don't have the data or the context to judge.

Second, we increasingly live in a society where many of us think that we are experts and good judges on many topics due to the vast amount of information that we have available through digital sources. However, too often we don't know what we don't know. We also base our decisions on too little information. To be a bit hyperbolic, you can't appreciate the dimensions of a leader's dilemma in 140 characters, nor can you provide a detailed judgment of your own in a space that small.

A third reason, is the issue discussed earlier, that setbacks and failures are part of the journey of being a leader. The longer perspective is the right way to judge a leader, not to make judgments of every small turn in the road. Often the time frame is too short. Decisions that seem poor today, may actually pan out over time (and vice versa).

When I speak on leadership, I often use examples from the US presidency since those people and their circumstances are well known (or should be known) to the general audience. I don't like to use examples from my own field because I don't want to hurt the feelings of my colleagues. Otherwise I would have to disguise the names and the places when I am using an example to make a point about leadership. One of the most interesting things to me about the history of the presidency is how the evaluation of a president evolves in the years after leave office. Historical perspective is often kinder (or crueler) than popular perception during their term of office. In 2008, I took my children with me when I went to vote in the Federal election. The older child asked me if I agreed with bumper stickers in the parking lot that referred to someone who wasn't running and said "worst president ever." I told my son two related things—first that historians (at least the good ones) benefit from reflection and prefer to withhold their judgment about presidential performance until years have passed and additional perspectives are gained. To try to lighten things up, the second thing I told him was that I thought from my own reading on the subject that it was a fairly competitive category with some other very strong contenders for the title of worst so I thought that time would tell. Most of the folks in line thought that this was pretty funny, except for few who probably were now insecure that someone had dared to question the strongly held opinion in their bumper stickers messages.

## HANDLING "FAILURE" AND ITS RISKS

My analogy here is to take this perspective with you going forward and to understand that being the head of a group or chair of a department will put you in the spotlight. Don't be surprised that you will be judged both hastily and at times incompetently. Medical professionals pay close attention to each other and are often judgmental in temperament. One of the tests of leadership is whether you can keep your focus while people are being overly critical, saying inaccurate things about you, rushing to judgment, etc. That shouldn't inhibit you from leading to the best of your ability and to have the courage to make mistakes along the way. Clearly you should still strive for perfection in your leadership role, just as you do when you are treating patients. However, you can't give in to fear or worry too much about what others will think. That is a recipe for failure as a leader. To paraphrase Lincoln, you can't make everyone happy and if you try you will not only fail in that goal, you will likely fail in your others.

## TRUE FAILURE AND ITS CONSEQUENCES

Sometimes failure really occurs and there aren't any quotes around it, ironic or otherwise. Academic chairs can be let loose before their terms are up and are getting fired in this generation. Medical groups lose contracts and their leaders may be let go as a result. Some groups dissolve in that situation and the leadership position disappears in the process. Tenured professors can lose their positions or have their job assignments altered unfavorably. Leaders of all sorts can have their responsibilities deliberately curtailed or be outright fired. Sometimes this is done quietly, sometimes in public. Usually, the language is softened and the publicity notice says that person in question has "resigned" to spend more time on personal pursuits, etc.

What do you do if you fail in public? Is your career over? Are you branded for life? Not necessarily. It depends on the circumstances. If the failure wasn't really your fault, discerning people might hire you anyway. Even if the failure was mostly your fault, in some sectors and in some circumstances that doesn't mean that your career is over or even that your career as a leader is over. In the entrepreneurial sector, where I previously worked many of the visionaries we worked with had somewhat checkered job histories. A previous business failure in a startup, at least in the United States, is not necessarily a detriment. In some cases it can even become a badge of honor—it says you are willing to take great risk and take on challenges that others would shy from.

In healthcare there is also hope. Many people land on their feet after a bad situation like getting fired. Let's look at some of the things that you can do after this happens:

1. Make sure that your networks are robust. You always need friends, but you particularly need friends when you are down. In fact, you will learn a lot about who your real friends are when this happens. The people who were your colleagues when you were at the top, but who shun you when you hit a rough patch will shake out quickly. Make sure that you reinforce the network connections you have and expand them.
2. Don't make this worse. If you are too hard on yourself or if you are too embarrassed to reach out to your mentors and friends then you will miss out on their help and may drive them away. Treat it for what it is—an experience that you can learn from and build on. Examine it, learn from it, and then move on. Replaying it repeatedly and reliving the past is unhealthy and will distract you from moving forward.
3. You need to develop an honest, intelligent set of responses to the questions that you will get about what happened. A smart thoughtful response that shows that you are a leader who can learn is probably your best approach. Blaming everyone else probably won't work. Every leader has to deal with good and bad people. Remember what we discussed earlier about taking responsibility for your decisions. Your failure may in fact be almost entirely someone else's fault, but taking responsibility for your share and discussing what you would

do differently will make you the kind of leader that someone would be willing to hire, rather than just seeing you as damaged goods.

4. Build on your strengths. Most of your professional colleagues have not had the chance to succeed or fail in a leadership role. Your experience, even if partly negative, is still very valuable and can give you insights that those who have only looked at leadership from the outside won't have. Someone interviewing you for a position that is comparable to your old one will probably be impressed with your ability to see issues that a naïve person would miss. Sometimes experience is an effective teacher.

There is an anecdote that is apropos here that I have always enjoyed sharing. A car executive decided to do an experiment on customer perception and loyalty. They decided to deliberately send out some cars with mild defects in them (presumably not the brakes!) and compare customer satisfaction compared to cars that were essentially perfect, that is, defect free. The customers with the defective cars were promptly called about the defect and the repairs were quickly made. The question at hand was which group was more satisfied with the company: the defect free customers or the repaired defect group. While the knee jerk response to this story is the defect free group, that isn't the answer in the usual telling of the story. Rather, sophisticated consumers know that cars are very complicated devices and that often defects turn up in course of several years of driving. The knowledge that these will be quickly and easily remedied trumps the delivery of a defect free vehicle. As much as most of us may obsess about any tiny blemish in our shiny brand new car, it is more important to know that things can and will be fixed by the merchant.

By analogy, the perfectionism that pervades our disciplines in healthcare may make some leadership failures terminal. That is unfortunate because there are many more failures in life that occur because people never try to lead. As the sports cliché goes (I first heard it in reference to ice hockey, but it has been appropriated by other sports as well), you miss 100% of the shots you don't take. Missing isn't the only way to lose and not trying may in fact be worse.

If I was considering you for a position after a leadership failure, I would not use that as a reason to not interview you. In fact, I would probably need an interview to make a decision. Compared to a "never leader" you have experience that may be very valuable. So many of the elements in the decision would depend on what happened, how you see it, what you learned, what your strengths are, etc. Another meme that has been taken out of context is F. Scott Fitzgerald's famous dictum that there are no second acts in American life. Its meaning is beyond the scope of this chapter, but it doesn't mean that people in America don't get a second chance. In any case, that is wrong. As I noted previously, in some sectors, this society can be very forgiving of failure and I see that as a strength, not a weakness.

## A FINAL THOUGHT

In considering the issues that surround the notion of failure in a career, one of my favorite anecdotes involves George Washington. Probably no citizen of the United States has been more lionized than Washington. However, in the apotheosis of this man in the American imagination, we often overlook the fact that by most counts he lost more battles than he won. He had more than his share of failures on the way to a genuinely revolutionary victory in the war for American independence. In your own situation, share the reasons for your failures with your group and keep moving forward. Remind them that winning the war is what matters and that we will have both ups and downs along the way. If you truly fail and lose your position, spend some time analyzing what happened and then get back in the saddle. Life is too short to dwell on failure.

## KEY POINTS

1. Great leadership involves courage, including taking measured risks.
2. As a leader be prepared for criticism even when it is short sighted and ignorant—this comes with the territory.
3. Be cautious in your own assessments of leaders. Unless you have a detailed understanding of their individual circumstances, you may be confusing luck (good or bad) with great strategic thinking.
4. Understand that the goal is to do the most good for your people and your institution during your tenure and that winning the war is more important than losing battles (at least some small ones) along the way.
5. Even failure—losing your job—doesn't have to be the end of your career. People do come back, even from big setbacks.

Image credit: Laozi, by Thanato; Wikimedia Commons

CHAPTER

# 21

# Becoming a Level 5 Leader

*"Change is coming"*
—John S. McCain, 2008 presidential campaign slogan, 1936-present

*change.gov*
—*name of the official website used by the then President-elect of the United States, Barack Obama, 2008*

## INTRODUCTION

As we have discussed at several points already, leadership becomes even more important in times of change. Change in the healthcare arena (and a lot of it, very quickly) was an idea that both major party candidates shared in the 2008 US presidential elections. By 2010, that change was law and since then has been implemented continuously. The ongoing ramifications will test our leadership in ways that few prior generations of medical workers could have imagined.

We not only need leaders to lead us through this period, we need good leaders. One of my favorite bumper stickers from my time in California was "Life is too short to drink bad wine." Our lives and our careers are too short to put up with incompetent or idiotic leaders. Just as leaders can have a disproportionately positive effect on an organization, then can also disproportionately hurt or even destroy an organization. Part of taking the mystery out of leadership is developing objective criteria for evaluating your leader or leaders. At the outset, let us separate leadership characteristics from simple numerical goals. Both are objectives, but there is a substantial difference in their use and their impact on decisions and outcomes.

In some institutions, the evaluation of a leader along with its attendant rewards (or penalties) is based upon quantitative external or internal goals. For example, your hospital administrator may get her end of the year bonus or her promotion based upon the hospital's bottom line economic performance for the year. The head of a sales team may get most

Leadership Lessons for Health Care Providers. http://dx.doi.org/10.1016/B978-0-12-801866-8.00021-4

or all of his compensation based upon the number of units that they sold or leased. Even in a not for profit, such as a zoo, the leader's compensation package can be tied to data, such as money raised, number of annual visits, membership renewals, or other objective criteria.

These examples, commonly used though they are, are not the kind of criteria we are going to discuss in this chapter. As we will see, those types of goals, while valuable, do not have the predictive impact that we need in times of rapid change. Instead, we are going to return to the Collin's system that was introduced earlier in this book because of the value that it has over the longer term in determining which leaders can work successfully in stressful times like these (see Lexa, 2009a).

It is important here to take a moment and clarify that the system involves both a person and a position. Someone may have what it takes to be a Level 5 leader but be stuck in a position where they can't exercise their abilities. Some medical professionals may be in positions where their job gives them little or no opportunity to develop a vision for their institution—or at least not until they move up to somewhere else in the organization. Since our topic in this section is the evaluation of those now in leadership positions, we will use a working assumption that our current leaders—the ones we are evaluating—are in positions where they can achieve Level 5 leadership.

We are then going to apply Collin's criteria to these leaders to understand what it takes to be an outstanding leader and ask the hard questions about why we don't have enough of them in healthcare, at least not yet.

## EVALUATING A LEADER: COLLIN'S LEVELS OF LEADERSHIP

Let's start with a quick review of Collins' system for levels of leadership (Collins, 2001). We will skip Level 1 (merely a highly capable individual) and Level 2 (a contributing team member). For the general definition of leadership, these "levels" are really just desirable employees, not people who should have designated leadership roles or positions in your organizations and who don't have high level leadership responsibilities. For example, a great nurse who is contributing to the work of the hospital but doing little else is a Level 1 leader. Someone who shows more initiative, helping his or her colleagues to improve their productivity, and to achieve the group's objectives is now demonstrating Level 2 leadership characteristics even though they may not have people who directly report to them or who they have to manage.

For the remainder of the discussion we will focus on the Collins levels that are more apt for those who can or should be in designated leadership roles. This ranged from: competent managers (Level 3), effective leaders

(Level 4) up to true executives (Level 5). Here are some details for each of these levels.

## Level 3: Competent Manager

This is a leader who "organizes people and resources toward the effective and efficient pursuit of predetermined objectives". This is the stereotype of the person posted in a middle management position in a typical Fortune 500 company. They manage a group or team toward objectives that are set by others, elsewhere in the firm, usually above them. These are often the types of annual goals we discussed in the introduction. Their job and their performance ratings are based upon how well they meet or exceed those goals and objectives. In healthcare, that might mean reducing waiting time for a hospital test by a certain amount of time this year, which would cut operating costs by 10% in this fiscal year. The person in this role may still have a fair amount of latitude in how they decide to meet the objectives and that is part of the boundary between this level and the one above and below. This would be a practice leader or other type of leader who takes direction from someone else, such as a Dean or hospital administrator and meets that person's objectives, rather than developing a personal vision for the group or department that they nominally lead.

## Level 4: Effective Leader

This is a leader who "catalyzes commitment to and vigorous pursuit of a clear and compelling vision, stimulating higher performance standards" The key differentiator from the next lower level is the element of vision—the difference between meeting a predetermined goal and creating a vision of where the organization needs to go and then getting commitment from your team. This is the chairman or president who has an independent vision for the practice—where it needs to go and can rally the troops to improve their performance and where necessary make changes to achieve it.

## Level 5: The Executive

This is the type of leader that we should aspire to be and/or have at the helm in our organizations. This person "builds enduring greatness through a paradoxical blend of personal humility and professional will." A Level 5 leader is the kind of executive who can put their own ego second to that of the institution. Sometimes people read this and misinterpret this to mean that they are not ambitious leaders. That misses the point that the personal ambition is subsumed into their drive for the success of the institution that they head. This is unfortunately the rarest form of leadership. Another way to think of this is to think how a charismatic Level 4 leader both helps an organization while simultaneously limiting its growth. As long as the organization can't grow past the ego of the leader, that provides a limit to progress and change in the organization. This distinction is important. I have seen enough hospital leaders and other medical leaders at this point to grasp the importance of this distinction. The growth opportunities for the group and for its members are much greater under a Level 5 leader. The rare combination of intense will and personal humility in these leaders can take groups to heights that other individuals could never reach.

Instead, the very best leaders understand that their personal ambitions will be met when the organization succeeds, not when their own egomania and narcissism is fulfilled. The first time I came across some of these concepts was in a text a bit older that the one that we are using in this chapter, but it is one we have encountered before. In the Chinese classic, *Tao Te Ching*, also known as the Book of the Way (attributed to Lao Tzu, 600–531 BC), there is a memorable quote on leadership "A leader is best when people barely know he exists, when his work is done, his aim fulfilled, they will say: we did it ourselves." This is the extreme opposite of the leader who creates crises that she/he can then heroically solve. It is a form of leadership that is as valuable as it is uncommon.

## APPLICATION

Within your organization, examine where your leaders are now. Ask the questions: is this the right person to lead? and can they become a more effective leader? Ask yourself if they can and most importantly: are they Level 5 material? In your practice, examine who can do that and take a hard look at your institution to see if there are environmental or organizational changes that you can make in order to open up the opportunity (if necessary) to make higher level leadership possible. Always remember that both the position and person matter here. Try to figure out if the limiting factor is the person, the position, or both and then look at what you can do to make the situation better.

## CLOSING

Great leadership is both precious and rare. In these times of rapid change in our field, there will be significant challenges to the current practice and the very future of our profession is at stake. Great leadership is not a luxury, but a necessity in times like these.

## KEY POINTS

1. Have the courage to evaluate your leaders.
2. Use objective criteria and goals.
3. Look at both the person and the position. Sometimes in our fields we jump to blame the person, when in fact it may be that the position is constructed in a way that limits a leader's ability to lead.
4. Ask is your leader (or leaders) at Level 5 performance? If the answer is no, why not?
5. Find, encourage, and facilitate Level 5 leadership in your organization in both yourself and in others.

*Image credit: Mount Rushmore; Wikimedia Commons*

# Choosing Greatness in Leadership

*"Forget about likes and dislikes. They are of no consequence. Just do what must be done. This may not be happiness but it is greatness."*
—George Bernard Shaw, Irish play writer and 1925 Nobel Prize of Literature, 1956-1950

## INTRODUCTION

In previous chapters, I referenced one of the seminal business books of recent years: *Good to Great,* by Jim Collins (2001). In this chapter, we will look at a more recent book called *Great by Choice* (Collins and Hansen, 2011). This work analyzes the characteristics of the leadership as well as other key factors in companies that outperformed their industries by at least 10-fold over two decades or more. Consider the impact of that sentence—doing ten times better than your closest competitors... Imagine that your hospital outperformed its major competitor an order of magnitude. What if its profitability were 10× the average—think of the equipment you could get, the amenities you could have for your patients, etc. What if your surgeons, your nurses, your radiologists, or your emergency department were ten times better than the nearest competitor? Imagine... There is a wealth of insight in this tome, but I want to focus on the authors' perspectives on key aspects of leadership in difficult times.

One of the first myths regards risk taking and vision. There is a highly prevalent myth that successful leaders are always brash (and rash) risk takers with unique visions. These are attractive stereotypes—the outsider who turns the world upside down by seeing what everyone else has missed and lives life on their terms, not societies. When portrayed in Hollywood, this usually includes riding motorcycles, having state of the art electronics, breaking the rules with impunity, and living in a cool house fit for a Bond villain.

Leadership Lessons for Health Care Providers. http://dx.doi.org/10.1016/B978-0-12-801866-8.00022-6

While there certainly have been geniuses who have succeeded in the corporate world and who also do (at least in part) fit the aforementioned description, they are more the rarity in our culture. While that is perhaps unfortunate, it is more often the case that the lone wolf inventor may not have the skills to run a company. In fact, often the purported "visionary" leader is merely an unrealistic narcissist who not only doesn't have a vision that can be realized, but even if he or she did have a great vision they still wouldn't be the right person to lead a group toward it.

Having an idiosyncratic view of the world has many advantages, but it may also be a serious impediment to succeeding in the marketplace. The extreme risk taker may just be foolish. Sometimes with luck they may succeed, just as some gamblers (albeit the minority) return from Las Vegas richer than they came. However, long-term business success is built upon innumerable decisions, time points, and factors. The chance that you will be lucky hundreds or thousands of times in a row is very low. Being lucky is great, but your blind luck will run out during your career if you don't also have the skills and the smarts. While some people may live life by the credo that it is better to be lucky than smart, the best case is to be both and in fact most people who are chronically successful have a share of both ingredients.

In the work published by Collins and Hansen, they found that the leaders who won (and beating your industry by 10-fold is truly a remarkable win, so this is a robust definition) were not more creative or bold than their matched controls. Instead they were more disciplined, more empirical, and more paranoid about things like risks and competition and changing markets. Next, we will go through this interesting, albeit perhaps counterintuitive result point by point.

## THREE KEY DIFFERENTIATING POINTS

### Discipline

The first point we will examine in greater detail is discipline. By this the authors mean the consistency and determination to stick to your core values and succeed. Many of us have had the experience of the opposite form of leadership—one that changes with wind. Every new fad that the hospital administrator or the local leader hears about gets implemented regardless of its value. I once worked with someone who changed their management style every time they picked up a new self-help book in an airport shop. These "manage your way to success" books have short half-lives and often these ideas have already begun to be discredited in the academic world and in the marketplace by the time that they wash up on the shores of the popular business literature. Anyone who reduces business success to three easy steps is probably kidding you and maybe is delusional themselves.

At best, this superficial form of leadership is distracting and at worst confounds your ability to stay on course and get the right things done. This is not to say that you can lead without flexibility. All of us need to adjust our plans to changing realities. The profound point here is what is at the foundation of your vision. Do you have values and significant goals for your department/practice or are you just improvising, throwing things against the wall, trying to see what sticks and hoping against hope to succeed? This first point is that one of the keys to great leadership across the spectrum, from government, military, corporate, and academic settings is disciplined, serious leadership. Just being a smart gal or guy and trying hard isn't enough. Improvisation and flexibility are also important, but if you are just doing improve you belong to a comedy club, not the "C" suite.

## Empirical Creativity

The second point is one of realism, but with an intellectual component. The authors noted that the successful leaders practiced what the authors called "empirical creativity." This could be summarized as a willingness to look at the environment and at data and see what others had missed. This is a very interesting point that encompasses two important ideas. First is the willingness to mine through data and find the gold that others have missed. Second is the courage to debunk conventional wisdom and to act upon it. One of the most tiresome forms of pseudo-leadership is the mere prattling and repetition of what is held to be conventional truth. The leader who feels smart because they can repeat what they read in a leading newspaper or have heard on the radio on their way to work or were sent in an email or short messaging format isn't practicing what these authors describe. Instead, the authors' observation about success is that it is the person who goes deep into the evidence—the empiricism—who is likely to win. This requires a rare combination of determination, analytic skills, creativity, and scepticism to be able to find opportunities that are both novel and important. Those are the types of opportunities that lead to real change.

## Healthy Paranoia

The third point involves paranoia—not of the debilitating clinical form, but rather a productive anticipation of problems. This is a key factor in success that we have discussed before in this column, the ability of the leader to think strategically and anticipate crises and problems. The ability to think at least a step or two ahead of the competition and act on it is a compelling success factor. One of the enduring lessons for individuals and organizations is that you need to be constantly vigilant for threats.

The paradoxical issue for many people is that the riskiest time is often when you are successful. You become "fat and happy" and lose the ability to imagine that this could all end for you. You lose sight of the dictum we discussed earlier that the future has no obligation to be kind to us. We need to anticipate the future and mitigate the risks as well as capture the opportunities. A great economist once observed that in dynamic economies, rapid progress is built upon "creative destruction" (Schumpeter, as quoted in The Concise Encyclopedia of Economics).

This is a two edged sword and it is a continuing process. The opportunities that led to your success can just as easily be replaced by opportunities for others that will in turn threaten you. This can happen to you quickly so you have to be vigilant in your paranoia. This is the reason that great leaders (and great organizations) are constantly vigilant for threats. In our case, we have more than our share, from working with a bankrupt government to disruptive technologies and turf battles, to name just a few. Great leadership requires a careful read of the observations of these authors.

## KEY POINTS

1. Great leadership need not be mysterious. It can be analyzed and there are patterns that we can learn from.
2. Great leaders are disciplined and apply principles to their leadership practice to be able to stick to their core value and goals.
3. Great leaders are pragmatic yet creative, using real world data but developing creative insights to see what others are missing.
4. Great leaders don't become satisfied and lazy—they keep up a healthy paranoia about what can go wrong, as well maintain vigilance against the threats to their current and continued success.

*Image credit: Meeting of the Executive Committee of the National Security Council, 29 October 1962, by Cecil W. Stoughton*

# 23

# Winning in a Crisis

*"Never let a good crisis go to waste"*
**—Winston Churchill, British statesman and twice Prime Minister of the United Kingdom, 1951-1955**

## INTRODUCTION

In our earlier chapter on crises, I considered an overview of the issues at stake in crisis leadership and the predictable temporal phases of crisis leadership. In this one, we return to the topic to go more deeply into crisis management and focus on those factors that can help leaders perform well in the pressure and confusion of a crisis and succeed in difficult times.

Again, I will start out by acknowledging that crises and their management take many forms. There are real crises that strike from without and threaten an organization. However, crises can also be used or exaggerated as we saw earlier or even manufactured to achieve political ends. The cliché "Never waste a good crisis" captures this opportunistic and at times cynical view as to how leaders both respond to and also act during crises. This reflects a core issue over ethical and unethical styles of leadership.

This point was forcefully made in a disturbing article appearing in *The Economist* that included an ironic discussion of the leadership style of Mao Tse-Tung (see "Mao and the art of management: a role model, of sorts"; available from: http://www.economist.com/node/10311230). One of the key leadership "lessons" of his "success" was having activity substitute for achievement. That form of "leadership" is a recipe for disaster, as anyone who survived Mao's "great leap forward" or the Cultural Revolution can attest. While Mao consolidated his power, millions of innocents suffered and died. Moreover as he rose to power he often mistreated those who had supported him along the way hurting them as well.

Instead, great leaders, as opposed to tyrants, should focus on achieving their goals during crises rather than just seeming busy while their

Leadership Lessons for Health Care Providers. http://dx.doi.org/10.1016/B978-0-12-801866-8.00023-8

organizations and constituents suffer. My focus today is on how ethical leaders cope effectively when crises arise, and I offer some advice on how they can make the best use of a bad situation.

## HANDLING A CRISIS: KEY POINTS FOR ETHICAL LEADERS

"Reason and calm judgment: the qualities especially belonging to a leader"
—*Publius Cornelius Tacitus, Senator and historian of the Roman Empire*

No leader, no matter how great, is immune to crises. Almost every leader will have their share. As we discussed earlier, even Prime Ministers and Presidents get their share and often much more. You need to be prepared for crises, you need to learn to lead in challenging circumstances and where possible you need to be able to turn the tables and not just live to fight another day, but in fact succeed in adversity.

Although it is both impossible and inappropriate to reduce leadership to a list of bullet points, there are many important ways that leaders should respond during a crisis. Failure to follow those rules can result in utter catastrophe or can significantly compromise a leader's performance during a challenging time. I explore several of the most important guidelines for crisis management in the subsequent sections.

### Manage Yourself First

As a healthcare leader, the first step you should take in a crisis is to maintain your own equilibrium: keep thinking and analyzing and don't let emotions overwhelm you. You may be angry and upset by the crises facing us in diagnostic imaging, but your success begins with managing yourself. You need a clear head to plan your response. An analogy here is running a resuscitation code in an emergency room or an intensive care unit: first, calm yourself down, and then you can focus on saving someone else's life. Panic leads to chaos and then to losing the battle.

### Maintain Your Focus

The next step in a crisis is to maintain your focus. When you are faced with losing a hospital contract, for instance, concentrate on the issue at hand and don't get distracted. The financial impact on your group, your choices, and the underlying reasons for the loss should all be in your sights. However, when stressed, some people can maintain focus and others tend to grasp at tangential issues. Airplane pilots are taught to always focus on flying the plane and deal with other issues on a secondary basis. If your passenger becomes ill, you first fly the plane, then do what you can to help. Aviation instructors will tell you that if a door pops open in flight, first fly the plane. If the plane has a malfunction or even a fire, you always continue to fly the plane while doing what you can to divide your time and attention to contain the damage. The key point is that if you become distracted and crash the plane, the other crises and issues become irrelevant (and likely so will you).

## Don't Just React and Play Defense; Plan Out A Winning Strategy for Weathering the Crisis

What we didn't cover in the early chapter is the jiu jitsu aspect of a challenge or crisis. When you are challenged or in a crisis, don't just react to an onslaught and go into survival mode; start to plan and implement a counterattack. A critical quality of successful leadership during the stress of a crisis lies in the ability to continue to think and plan strategically (see Weiss, 2002). If you are merely reacting, the other side has the advantage. Even when you are losing the battles, you can still be planning how to win the war. Going back to the George Washington example even as he was retreating, he was keeping the larger picture in mind. That is why we remember him as a winner. It is critical when you are under fire as the leader of your group that you remember to keep an eye on both the bigger picture and the future. Don't just respond; try to take the lead in seeing how you can make the best future that you can for you and your group.

## Map Out New Opportunities and Solutions

Use the crisis as an acid test of your current organization, your people, your technology, etc. Out of the stresses of the crisis, start rebuilding as soon as you can. To take it a step further than we did before, don't just use as time to reflect. A crisis in progress means that a lot changes may already be in play. A nimble leadership may be able to make long needed changes quickly with far less trauma than they would in more placid times. While it may seem farfetched when you are distracted by the crisis, try to think about the aftermath. What will be different, what opportunities will open up, how has the landscape changed, and how can you capitalize on this to build a better future for your department or group or service. Until you experience it, you may not believe that some of the best strategic planning occurs during times of great challenges. All of us would prefer to do our strategic planning and build our tactical plans during a quiet time in our office when we can put our feet up. Crises are the opposite. As I emphasize the silver linings in a crisis, one of them is that the immediacy of a crisis may jolt you into understanding issues in ways that you never would have otherwise.

## Use A Crisis Well

To take it a step further, sometimes crises are not merely bumps in the road but genuine opportunities for leading. Although the best time to make changes might have been before the storm, you should still make the best of the bad times. Changes that should be made at some point, can sometimes be done more easily when there are other big events afoot. For example, during a forced merger or a contract renewal or some other big difficult event, external forces may press you into making long needed changes in personnel, organizational structure, technology portfolio, geography or work schedule or some other important issue. A final point is that the storm will end, and you can be sure that there will be future crises, both those you can anticipate and those you cannot. Use the opportunity to hone your skills and those of your team to be ready for the next round.

## KEY POINTS

1. As soon as you can get some control in the crisis, move on and then focus on both the crisis and the bigger picture.
2. Crises are not merely obstacles; they can be great opportunities as well. Look for a winning play or plays in the midst of the chaos.
3. Find ways to play offense even when you are beset with problems. Merely reacting to a crisis is a recipe for a stalemate or even a loss.
4. Crises are opportunities to examine yourself and your institution. Use them to make things better and be ready for the next challenge.

*Image credit: Junior doctors' strike in 1975, by Tony Rao*

# 24

# Leading in Serious Conflicts

*"Huns only make enemies on purpose"*
*—Weiss Roberts, on describing Attila the Hun's diplomacy and politics*

*"The Pope! How many (military) divisions has he got?"*
*—attributed to Joseph Stalin in a conversation with Winston Churchill*

## INTRODUCTION

In the first chapter about conflict, we began a discussion of how to think about conflict and your role as a leader in handling disagreements and minor conflicts. The advice in that chapter can help you in preventing friction, not starting stupid fights, and in handling low-level disputes. However, in some situations, even the best efforts can't prevent an escalation toward serious conflict. The quotes that lead the column this quarter are good reminders of some of the many points that you should consider before marching into a battle. The first is good advice: don't make enemies unless there is no other course of action. No one should make an enemy by mistake. A clumsy act or ill-considered statement that creates an enemy accidentally is the act of a fool, not a seasoned leader. The second is a common freshman mistake—underestimating your opponent. Seasoned warriors know that that can be a critical or even existential error. There is nothing heroic about being stupid and doing damage to yourself and your organization. Always consider carefully all the types of hard (and soft) power that your opponent can use against you. While tank divisions would not have been the tiny Vatican state's strong suit in a conflict with the Red Army of the Soviet Union, the Pope could use the influence and soft power that derived from his millions of followers and relationships with other world leaders. What follows is a framework to help you make a strategic analysis of your situation at the onset of a conflict in terms that are suited to a conflict situation.

Leadership Lessons for Health Care Providers. http://dx.doi.org/10.1016/B978-0-12-801866-8.00024-X

## ASSESSMENT

The first step in a handling a conflict is to try consider all of your choices. You won't get them all, but use a framework to make sure that you cover most of them. Ask what caused the primary threat. Are there additional threats? In an analogy to the other types of crises is there an opportunity or even more than one in this crisis? Can you use the conflict to your advantage to weaken or even get rid of a foe who has been a chronic problem? Try to evaluate how and why you would escalate or de-escalate the conflict. For example, if this is a turf battle is this one that you can win and is it one that you need to win? Is there something that you can do in a trade to bring the conflict to a close? Is there a smarter outcome than win lose? In another example, if this is a nasty contract situation where two sides are locked in their positions, can you come up with a better solution for both sides than your opponent currently has in mind?

When I describe this in these terms, people who know tell me that it is analogous to being on a battlefield, so try to see the whole landscape and try to weigh the pluses and minuses of each potential course of action before you jump in. A common mistake that many leaders make is to just do what seemed to work the last time. If you have been following the advice from the rest of the book you should have taken time after your last difficult situation or crisis ended to sit down and analyze what you did right and what you did wrong. If you followed that advice, you should be able to look at the outcome and separate out what was due to luck and what was due to smarts. This time around use those lessons to aim to do better.

## ALLIANCES

To reiterate when you step into a conflict always take time to look at the whole field of play and always include all the players. Consider who is on your side and who is against you. One of the things that can be bewildering about healthcare to those who are not insiders like us is the plethora of stakeholders. The ones that matter in healthcare are legion, including patients, their families, organized patient groups, practitioners of all types, administrators, government regulators, and in some cases even vendors of medical products among others.

When a battle starts, whether its something as simple as benign snowball fight on a schoolyard all the way up to the real thing and pretty much everything in between, your first question should be who is on my side and who is on the other side.

In your next leadership challenge that involves conflict, you should ask that question. Then you need to go deeper and figure out who is a good ally and who is a weak ally, who is a strong opponent and who is weakly opposed to you, etc. Also, try to find out who will stay neutral and how can you and your opponent try to influence those people to change their positions. When I do consulting work with medical professionals, many of them have trouble separating their personal feelings from their rational evaluation of how other members of the hospital or medical school will react in a conflict. Sometimes the annoying surgeon who always belittles your staff in meetings by making snide remarks may actually be a strong potential ally in a tough situation with the hospital administration. Actions speak much louder than feelings.

On the other hand the friendly anesthesiologist who you flirt with in the cafeteria may turn out to be an implacable enemy when you and she find yourselves on opposite sides over a rough budgetary issue. You and your team need to make a cool, clear assessment of your allies and enemies before you enter into or escalate a conflict. One of my favorite quotations from the Art of War is that most battles are won (or lost) before they are fought. Try to remember that quote and make your decisions appropriately including your analysis of alliances, both actual and potential.

## PLANNING

Don't fight for the sake of fighting. Fighting per se and angry gestures in particular are a waste of time. Instead, when your opponent is acting out, try to be the better woman or man. Instead of getting drawn in, try to stay calm and treat conflict as a negotiation. Think about the core issues in a negotiation: What do you want? What do they want? How much can you each give up? What can't either of you give in on? What is their best alternative to a negotiated agreement (BATNA in the jargon of negotiation). Is there a creative solution, can you find a third way or is it just a zero sum game where one wins and the other loses? In most cases, a smart negotiator can find a better solution than those that were on the table at the start of a conflict. In fact, the smart development of novel options that are more palatable than the original choices in the conflict is one of the best outcomes in a disagreement that leads to conflict. Unfortunately in the heat of battle many of us are too distracted by our emotions and our worries to think clearly and calmly about smarter choices and better outcomes.

Consider how far you will go and what your best alternatives are. Would you really give up the contract? Do they know how far you will go? Would you really leave your department over this issue? Sometimes the worst outcomes in an organizational conflict occur because of profound misunderstandings by both parties. Neither of them accurately assesses which threats are real and which are bluffs. This leads to blundering that results in something worse than a win/lose outcome—a lose–lose result where both sides blunder into a worse situation than when they started.

The planning phase is often a test of your negotiating skills. Think about what you will give up on in a fight and what you absolutely cannot say yes (or no) to when you are at the negotiating table. It often helps to map out where you are and which outcomes would be acceptable. Like the Rolling Stones, song, you can't always get what you want—but you may get something you can live with, particularly if the alternative is nothing.

## HAVE AN EXIT STRATEGY

This leads ultimately to key element of smart fighting—have a goal (or goals) which includes an exit strategy. No one gains in an endless conflict. If you really are going to have a battle between your department and another hospital department then consider how you will stop it. That means that if you can, even before you start the conflict or at least as early as you can. There is a doctrine in US military thinking that is attributed to General Colin Powell that is a series of critical questions that need to be answered before a nation goes to war and one of them is exactly this—what is the exit strategy? (for further details, see http://en.wikipedia.org/wiki/Powell_Doctrine). Starting a war without considering this question can lead to terrible outcomes. For those of us in civilian life, this is an important insight that should guide our thinking about our much less intense battles and conflicts.

Part of this end game should include mending fences. Most of our conflicts in medical settings will occur with people and organizations with which we have had a long-term relationship and in many cases will continue to have a relationship. As soon as enough acrimony has dissipated to do so, you need to start winning the peace. Hopefully the escalation to conflict has encouraged you to build a stronger relationship and even turn your enemy into a friend or at least a neutral. It is also a good time to assess who your other friends and enemies were during the fight. You probably found out who your real friends were. Never forget that, it is invaluable.

## KEY POINTS

1. Don't start stupid fights and don't make enemies (except on purpose!).
2. Fights for the sake of fights are at best stupid and at their worst are very destructive to individuals and their groups. Only fight if you must and then beyond defending yourself try to fight for a reason or a goal. Have a plan for ending the conflict that includes the details: when, where, why, how, and who.
3. Within the fight, see it as a complex negotiation. While you will get emotional, try to stay as calm and cerebral and understand what you and your opponent are doing and when it is time to stop.
4. When the fighting stops, immediately work to repair the damage and to start working on preventing the next conflict.
5. Always learn from the situations that confront you as a leader. Always work relentlessly to learn so that you will do better.

*Image credit: President Reagan and Soviet General Secretary Gorbachev having their first meeting in the oval office at the White House, 8 December 1987*

# Leadership and Trust

*"Trust, but verify"*
**—Russian proverb used by President Ronald Reagan, referring to US nuclear arms negotiations strategies with the Soviet Union.**

## INTRODUCTION

Trust is one of the keys to success in social circumstances. If you don't trust your colleagues, your business partners, or your significant other, then you will either eventually sever the relationship or have to invest an inordinate amount of time and energy in order to verify that they are acting appropriately. Many of us who live in the United States are jealous of nations where the level of societal trust is higher and the freedom that it brings is greater. This was highlighted by a famous case from 1997 in New York City of a Danish woman who left her baby in a stroller on the sidewalk while she went into a restaurant; She was then arrested for putting her child at risk. In the course of the case the point was made that this was common practice in her home country (article available from: http://www.nytimes.com/1997/05/14/nyregion/toddler-left-outside-restaurant-is-returned-to-her-mother.html). Eventually the child was returned to her and in a further example of the consequences of lack of trust, and of living in a lower trust society, she went on to sue the city over this cultural misunderstanding.

Recently, I was watching an old movie with one of my sons and he noticed that as the protagonist left on a trip, he arrived at the airport with just a few minutes to go before a flight and was able to run right onto his plane. When he expressed his disbelief, I then froze the recording. I had to explain to him, that yes there was a time when we didn't have to stand in line in our socks to be X-rayed and patted down before we went on a vacation that involved air travel. Not a great example of how the world has

Leadership Lessons for Health Care Providers. http://dx.doi.org/10.1016/B978-0-12-801866-8.00025-1

progressed over the past few decades. Lack of trust can not only impede progress, but can also cause us to regress. Lack of trust can occur at levels from our personal relationships to the geo-political and creates enormous "dead weight" economic losses, financial friction, wastes of time, and all manner of other inefficiencies. To the extent we can in our leadership roles, we can and should nurture relationships of high trust to move forward in improving our organizations and our jobs.

## BUILDING TRUST AS A LEADER

In this chapter's discussion, we will look at the importance of building and increasing trust in your role as a leader. Trust (or its lack) is one of the measures of both your effectiveness and efficiency as a leader. If members of your organization and your key stakeholder groups trust you, then you will be able to accomplish much more and with both much greater efficiency and also a lower expenditure of resources to achieve your goals.

To make it clear before we go further, I want to answer some helpful criticism that I got from a friend on this topic. This section's intent is not to rehash the recurring arguments over whether or not it is better to be loved or feared as a leader or a nation. This can get tiresome and like many dichotomies it includes an healthy dose of falsehood. The right answer is it depends and can encompass both in different circumstances, but isn't either/or. The US Marines have a slogan of "your best friend and your worst enemy" which succinctly answers the debate over love and fear with "both." Trust is a different issue that goes into a more concrete and rationale domain—can I trust you to do what you say or do I need to use frequent monitoring, teams of lawyers, and other wasteful endeavors to make sure that you will do what you promise.

An article by Robert Hurley (2011) provides a nice summary of the value of trust in an organization and what the determinants of a trusted leader are. As he begins the article, he points out trust is associated positively with many key objective factors of organizational success, such as revenue, profitability, returns to investors, and employee turnover. He breaks down trust issues into five principles that leaders need to follow in order to build trust in themselves and their organizations. We will go through them and discuss their applications in healthcare settings.

1. **Show that your interests are the same.** Trust depends upon awareness that there is a common ground. This is critical both internally and externally in an organization. If you are leading a group of professionals like yourself, you need to *all* share together

in both the good and bad outcomes of your common work and decisions. People will not trust a leader who doesn't do her or his share of the work or who takes more than their share of the rewards. That is not to say that groups should fail to reward their leaders fairly for their leadership time and efforts, they absolutely have to do that to get good leaders and help them succeed. That has been covered previously in this space and we will certainly return to it in the future. That said though, it is critical that everyone's interests be aligned within the group and that the share of work done by the leadership is fairly distributed.

It may be hard for some readers to understand that this is just as important with your other stakeholder groups. While trust within your group is important it is the start not the end. The same principles work as you work outward centripetally from your department, practice or group or division into the relationships that you have with other stakeholders. This is not always well appreciated, particularly by those who have developed an "us and them" mentality. Part of this may be due to popular depictions of business on media, such as television and film that often focus on "zero sum" forms of negotiations—aggressive, heated meetings between sides that turn into winners and losers depending on how much of a pie that they get. While those negotiations certainly do occur in real life and they do make for good drama, what is interesting to me is how often it is not the norm. Many successful negotiations result instead from finding common ground and searching out ways that both parties can come out reasonably well or even ahead—the so-called "win–win" outcome. While it won't happen every time, there are negotiations where both parties find value together that they hadn't contemplated separately. This requires savvy, smart negotiators who build trust and value their ongoing relationship.

If you can find ways to interact with your other healthcare departments that build upon common interests you can find winning outcomes and avoid the turf battling, name calling, and stereotyping that has become so destructive in some medical facilities in the United States. This is even worse than a "win/lose" outcome. In many cases, this is really a "lose/lose" result. People who are keeping score are settling for an "I lose less and you lose more" as an end result. This may sound utterly irrational to someone who has never seen it happen, but it is occurring and is a disturbing aspect of low/ no trust relationships. No one benefits from that and it wastes time, money, and goodwill at a time when we need all those things for other endeavors in healthcare. Furthermore, it poisons the relationship between the negotiating parties and sets up a situation where it is very likely that the next negotiation will also be as bad or perhaps worse. Instead, we need to build better relationships with other stakeholders all through the list from our patients to administrators and government officials.

2. **Demonstrate your concern.** Leaders need to show that they can be trusted to do the right thing. In your case, consider how you treat people and look for ways to build trust with them. If you have to make a difficult decision about salary or call, be as fair and as transparent as you can. If you are asking the group to make a sacrifice, you as a member of the group should be sacrificing too. Many leaders act as if they are separate from the group. Rather, as the leader, you need to be a role model and do at least your part for the group in sharing in hardship. This is not just the humane thing to do, it is also the only way that you can be effective. If your group doesn't believe that you care, they will not support you and everyone will suffer. Make sure they know that you understand their situation and try to ameliorate the burden when you can.

3. **Deliver on your promises.** I know that an admonition about keeping promises may sound trite to many readers. When I advised one leader that the reason that their hospital contract was in jeopardy was due to broken promises, he was taken aback. He thought that he was just being an aggressive leader and getting as much as he could from the hospital. What he failed to see was that broken trust had resulted from his failure to keep his promises. His poor track record and untrustworthiness had made the hospital look for alternatives and had also raised the administrators costs of verifying that contract was being fulfilled. In the end, this person had only been fooling himself with a mistaken notion of what makes a great leader.

Now I am not saying not to make promises, but I would say be very careful about what you promise people—you may forget, but they almost never will. A broken promise to a colleague will make them always question your ethics, your judgment, and ultimately whether they will want to continue to be associated with you. When I walk through the halls of the top medical meeting in my field each year in Chicago, much of the negative gossip about leaders focuses on issues of trust: leaders who don't keep promises, who lie, who are otherwise "ethically challenged" as the euphemism goes or even worse.

The message here is twofold—make promises carefully, but stand and deliver when you do make a promise. If you have to break a promise, then do it as fairly as you possibly can. It is more than a little unfair to break a promise about a raise to one of your younger colleagues while you pocket a hefty incentive bonus. If you have to break a promise, explain your reasons, apologize, and try if you can to try to make amends for the infraction. You may brush it off and forget it, but have no doubt that the injured is not going to forget the hurt that this caused and is likely to share that story with as many of their closest friends and colleagues as they can.

4. **Be honest.** Again this may seem to some readers like advice from kindergarten, but the complexities and pressures of modern life seem to cause many people to hide behind half-truths and outright lies in their practices and departments. It doesn't help that there has been a degradation of attention to truth in our culture. Much of our news is "spun" or slanted by those who would sell us agendas rather than provide us with real news, let alone the truth. This is a reminder that for leaders to be chronically successful they need to be trustworthy and telling the truth is a core part of that. You need to strive for consistency, stability, and honesty. No one is perfect and when you, or someone in your organization does make mistakes, don't cover up and lie. Instead, be honest and fix what you can. Healthcare professionals are smart, so lying to them and then pretending that you didn't do it is a double hit. You lied and now you are treating the injured party like an idiot. They aren't fooled and you shouldn't act like a fool.

5. **Communication.** The last principle is about maintaining communication. A failure to communicate honestly and clearly is often at the root of both real conflict and suspicions that lead to imagined slights which then in turn can lead to genuine conflicts. Work hard at keeping people up to date on the issues that the group faces internally as well as with important stakeholders who are external to your group. These issues have been important in the past and will be critical as healthcare providers enter now into ACOs or ACO-like entities in the future. Hiding information or even the perception of hiding information can be poisonous in a high trust relationship like those that many of us have in healthcare. You have to keep some things confidential in the course of your work, but make sure that you are communicating regularly and well with your colleagues and that you can justify your secrecy when you think that it is needed.

## KEY POINTS

1. Trust is one of the key sources of power and success in leadership.
2. Align your interests with those you lead.
3. Show people that you are interested and concerned for their well being.
4. Make promises carefully and then deliver.
5. Consistency, honesty, and clear communication skills are hallmarks of a trusted leader.

*Image credit: Ethics Ideals Principles Morals Standards Concept*
*© Rawpixel.com/shutterstock*

# 26

# Principled Leadership

*"We choose to go to the moon. We choose to go to the moon in this decade and do the other things, not because they are easy, but because they are hard, because that goal will serve to organize and measure the best of our energies and skills"*
**—John F. Kennedy, 35th President of the United States, 1961-1963**

## INTRODUCTION

One of the oldest arguments about leadership focuses on whether or not it is possible for leaders to be both successful and ethical. Can they follow principles in a highly competitive world or do they need to play dirty, bend rules, cut corners, etc. in order to win? As the second decade of the 21st century opens, people across nations, cultures, and industries are suspicious that winners—particularly in business and finance—are guilty until proven innocent. As the world recovered from what is now being termed the "Great Recession" there was a strong sentiment that principles and ethics have had little to do with successful leadership. While there is some truth in this viewpoint, the world has never been completely black nor white. Furthermore, since I've worked with my share of the ethically challenged, I don't have illusions that cheaters always lose and that principled individuals always win.

Let's acknowledge here that there is some good news and some bad news. The bad news is that we do live in imperfect world. The good news is that if you are old enough to read this book, you already knew that. In the short term, sometimes bad behavior succeeds. However for those of you who adhere to religious, moral, and/or ethical values in your work life, there is a silver lining in this discussion. Longer term success is more likely for leaders who adhere to principles and can follow through with them.

**Leadership Lessons for Health Care Providers. http://dx.doi.org/10.1016/B978-0-12-801866-8.00026-3**

## START WITH STEWARDSHIP

In considering what guiding principles you should lead with, begin with the long view. If you are looking to leave a legacy, you will seek principles that take you along the high ground. People who can only think about short-term gains and who are looking out only for themselves are more likely to look for short cuts and break rules if they think that they can get away with it. However, if you consider yourself a steward of a worthy enterprise or institution then your concerns will include that legacy. If you are a proud member of an honored profession then maybe you feel peer pressure from those colleagues you have in the present, and in some cases a sense of honor that extends from the past and into the future to do the right thing and uphold those values. Preserving and protecting that long-term value is not only more difficult, but also much more rewarding than just a short-term gain. If you begin with a lofty goal like stewardship in mind at the beginning of the journey you are more likely to be successful in staying on track as you move through your tenure as a leader.

## LEADING WITH A PLAN VERSUS FAKING IT

A culture of principled decision making will also be a bulwark when the hard decisions arise. Every leader is eventually confronted with situations that fall into the gray zones. Every time that I go to a major medical meeting, I hear stories from leaders in our field who are facing things that they felt they weren't prepared for. All of us struggle with things that weren't in our training, our classes, or any text book. Occasionally, the right answer is also the easy one—ask your human resources expert or your lawyer. In many circumstances, however, those people can only advise and you still have to sweat it yourself. The problem is still on your shoulders. Having guiding principles is the only way to get past the "faking it" style of some leaders. Principles should be part of your plan and your vision. As we have already discussed many times, leaders need to have both a vision and plans. Grown up, highly trained professionals can't just come into work and "wing it" and hope that they will succeed. They need to work from foundational principles. The stress of the times that we are now living through makes it almost impossible to thrive for very long without detailed planning and principle-based leadership. This will guide you in the dark times. If someone tries to pressure you to substitute a cheaper, but worse drug for a patient, will you do the principled thing or the expedient?

## THE LEADER IS SPECIAL

Former NBA star, Charles Barkley once said "I'm not a role model... Just because I dunk a basketball doesn't mean I should raise your kids." This is a great quote, because it is both honest and self-deprecating while also being very, very smart. Unfortunately in our culture, not enough people are listening to Mr. Barkley's wise advice. While some politicians and sports stars do make remarkably bad role models, for better or worse most such leaders are held up as exemplars to youth in particular and to society in general. At the personal level, this is also true for you in your group/department. As the leader, your peers and other personnel will look at your example. This is particularly true of moral and ethical guidance. If you are seen as unethical and hypocritical, then you shouldn't be shocked when that behavior starts to permeate your organization from other people's actions. Professionals are supposed to have a strong internal compass, but there is still a strong tendency even among seasoned professionals to look around and see what the leadership is doing. If the rules are bent by those on the top, the outcomes are likely to all be at risk. Usually this is a combination of either becoming profoundly cynical and dysfunctional or following the leader down the slippery slope of bad actions until someone really goes over the line and does serious damage to themselves and others.

Since you can't possibly oversee every decision in your organization, you should be very concerned about the ethical culture in your institution. As a leader, you are setting that tone and example for everyone. You may not like that role but be advised it comes with the job. People will pay close attention to you whether you like it or not. Be concerned about small infractions because this may lead to other people doing ever more questionable acts. As a leader, you will have to clean up the messes if your members do things that go over the line. Remember every day that you are setting an example. You may resent this added pressure in your role, but it comes with the territory.

## WHO DO YOU TRUST?

Leading by example and using principles to guide your professional life are essential to successful leadership. As we said at the opening, other than nasty dictatorships, most groups are built on elements of trust and your trustworthiness as a leader is the cornerstone of building a team that can win. All groups require commitment and many expect some form of sacrifice. Because of their dedication, many healthcare professionals show remarkable degrees of sacrifice. They often work long and irregular hours. They cover for each other and take rough on-call schedules. Healthcare professionals put themselves in harms way regularly as they take care of the sick. This is only possible if the leader has the integrity to inspire trust and confidence in the rest of the group.

Here I would share several pieces of hard won wisdom that I have both learned myself the hard way as well as have heard repeatedly from many leaders in our field. First, we discussed it before, but it is worth expanding on this discussion since it bears on trust and principles. Remember to be careful what you promise. Of all the sins of leaders, one of the worst is to break a promise to colleague. You will be seen as either a liar or a fool. How you handle it determines which of those predominate, but either way you have blundered very badly. The second is that this shouldn't make you overly cautious, that is, wandering through life never making bold plans. Great leaders need to make promises. The greatest are remembered for making the biggest promises. I suspect that deep into the future one of the things that the United States will be remembered for most is that it was the first space faring nations to take humans to the Moon and fulfill the President's promise. Finally, when you stick to your principles and have a setback, remember that all great leaders do fail from time to time. Failure shouldn't be the endpoint. You need to move forward, explain, be honest, and start to rebuild. In difficult times, I am reminded of the quote from JFK that opens this column. Doing great things is obviously usually quite hard, but that is the point and that is why they are worth it.

## KEY POINTS

1. Leadership is not just a set of activities, it is also about vision and character.
2. Principles matter: for you, for your coworkers, and for the group/ institution that you serve.
3. Building and maintaining trust isn't merely a good thing to do or the right thing to do. It is also the key to being able to do great things and one of the keys to making business relationships more effective and less costly. In short, it is also a smart thing.
4. Individuals and groups can only succeed through a climate of commitment and trust. Your integrity and principled leadership are the cornerstone for building an effective team.
5. Following principles doesn't mean that you will win every time, but having a plan and sticking to it even in tough times is strong element of long-term success.

*Image credit: Apollo 11 plaque, NASA; Wikimedia Commons*

# 27

# Motivation and Leadership

*"The beatings will continue until morale improves"*
—**Pirate themed office cartoon**

## INTRODUCTION

One of the managerial battles of my generation of physicians has been over productivity. During the digital transition in medicine, we have been encouraged, incentivized, and in some cases even threatened in order to get us to do more work in less time. While the transition to electronic records, to picture archiving and communication systems, and to voice recognition was difficult for those who had trained in the analog era, ultimately these IT systems have allowed a significant growth in how much work those of us in medical imaging could do. At face value that is obviously a good thing, but this revolution, like most revolutions, has its downsides. The transformation has also led to negatives, such as battles over which of us did more or less of this higher volume of work, the faster rate of work crowds out other tasks, such as taking the time to teach, to do research, or other important work. There was and still is the downside of reducing time for human interaction as people are hunkered down in front of computer screens rather than talking to each other, doing consultations, and answering the phone.

My friends in other areas of medicine have experienced their own productivity battles as they are pressured to see more patients, cover more beds, do anesthesia and surgical procedures faster, turn the ED beds over quickly, etc. Many physicians and nurses complain of being treated like they are automatons or line works in a factory. As cost pressures rise and as the population gets older and probably sicker as well, we will be almost certainly under more pressure to work harder. The assembly line analogy is commonly used to describe this, but if you know much about the history of the assembly line it should give you pause. Like many stories from

Leadership Lessons for Health Care Providers. http://dx.doi.org/10.1016/B978-0-12-801866-8.00027-5

history there is more than one side to the narrative. Those productivity increases came with costs.

Henry Ford is often given credit for developing the modern assembly line in his car factories. In fact, the core concept was probably adapted from several other types of assembly plants, but most interesting is that it was inspired in part by the work layout of a slaughterhouse. Obviously there the task was to disassemble or deconstruct rather than to construct something but the story may be true. More important though to our discussion is the observation that many of the early employees found the automobile factory work deadening. It paid much better than farm work which was in fact an early source of workers and also paid better than some other kinds of industrial labor of the time, but it was hard, repetitive, boring work. For many who were looking for an interesting job in the exciting new world of the automobile, they instead did the same small task over and over again. The turnover rate for workers was high as many native born Americans left the lines after trying it but finding that they couldn't keep up. One of the reasons why the Detroit metropolitan area has such a diverse population is that Ford encouraged both domestic migration and international immigration to keep its factories running with fresh workers to replace those who couldn't or wouldn't continue.

In healthcare, the important questions on this topic should begin with whether treating those of us in the caring professions like factory workers makes sense. Does it work? Does paying productivity bonuses actually work? Do you get more and/or better work out of nurses and physicians if you pay them that way? Do they instead cut corners and/or does quality go down as workloads go up? Does the converse—using punishments for low productivity motivate people or do they become discouraged and lower their performance along other metrics, such as service, friendliness, etc.?

The doubts about using money and other inducements to change health worker behavior come from both the literature and from my work in consulting with healthcare practices. In my own work, I have seen leaders and managers experiment with motivational schemes that involve money or time off or both. To put it charitably, the results are mixed. They often succeeded in the short term in getting the behaviors that they wanted, but the healthcare workers often cut corners elsewhere or let other things go in order to make time to do the things that were rewarded.

This is not unique to my experiences nor is it unique to healthcare. There is an interesting succinct book called *Drive* by Daniel Pink (2011) that explores what is known about what motivates (and also what demotivates) knowledge workers. It includes references to the literature in this subject so it is worth a read if you are struggling with this hard topic.

# WHAT DO YOU WANT TO MOTIVATE

At first glance, the behaviors you want to motivate in your colleagues may not seem that dissimilar to the factory line worker. You want people do a lot of work and you want them to do it right. In both cases, mistakes are costly, so you don't want people to get sloppy. The difference though is that healthcare is more complicated, much more complicated. There are far more variables, a great deal more uncertainty and dimensions of risk and service and stakeholder groups that don't have very good analogs in the factory setting. If you motivate someone with simplistic mechanisms, they have lots of ways to lose focus, to cut corners, to be distracted, and to be sloppy.

In healthcare, as we have discussed elsewhere in this book, you have many customers. If you push a nurse or doctor to go too fast, they may not take the time to talk with their colleagues, or with family members. They may get their charting done, but not discuss a hard case with a coworker. Using sticks and carrots with healthcare workers can lead to unexpected or even perverse outcomes. Many times when I am asked to consult with a leader about motivating their workers, the leader begins the conversation by asking questions about tactics in motivation, that is, which carrots and sticks should I use and when. That is the wrong way to begin, since it begins with an often false assumption. The assumption is that people aren't working hard enough The right way is to first discuss what are the productivity goals and what tradeoffs you might be willing to accept. The strategy or strategies you come up should be robust and clearly aligned with what you want to achieve. Once you figure out that then you can move on to tactics and implementation. What follows is a framework and a format that I often use in these cases that includes steps in the process and some suggestions for avoiding serious mistakes when you do this.

# IS THERE REALLY A PROBLEM AND HOW IMPORTANT IS IT?

The first step is assessing if there is a genuine problem. If there is a problem, next decide if it is big enough to justify changing your policies and procedures or is it a small issue that you should just keep an eye on? In my own field of radiology, it became common several years ago to focus on the productivity of individual radiologists. This often took the form of measuring number of studies read per year or RVUs (relative value units) per year. I would get a call from a group that was having conflicts over how hard people were working. At the time they were mostly internal, but occasionally were driven by an individual or organization outside the group. When I then met with the leader, one of my first tier questions to him or her would be to suggest that we go over the data. In many of the early cases, there wasn't any. It was a matter of perception—"so and so" takes too long a lunch or is on the phone a lot, etc. The perception was that because "so and so" was doing other things then they must not be doing their share. It was interesting that often these perceptions were not only wrong, but sometimes very wrong. It would often turn out that the accused slacker was actually outperforming the group average and often their accuser. As a leader you need to tread into this arena carefully.

The lesson here is that the first job is to get the data. The second is to make sure that the data are good. In some work that I was doing with a surgical group, these issues were at the center of a conflict within the group that threatened to bring them apart. At face value, there were substantial disparities in the number of cases (yes I am leaving out details like the type of surgery to protect confidentiality) that made it appear like some people were doing a lot more. On closer inspection, there were clear elements in the data that showed that some of the surgeons were taking on patients who were substantially sicker and more complicated than the others and that it was captured well in the data that they were using in their fights. Once those important modifiers were factored into the analysis, it was clear that that explained the disparities and that everyone really was working hard to the point of doing their share and that the residual differences were both small and within a reasonable margin of error. Overreacting in the absence of good data is clearly a mistake, but worse it can be a mistake with severe consequences. It may rupture the bonds of trust in the group and worse take you down a path where your decision ultimately gets debated by experts in front of a jury. Make sure that the data are solid before you make your move.

## WHAT DO I WANT TO ENCOURAGE AND WHY?

The aforementioned last example drives home the issue of perverse incentives driving perverse outcomes. If you only reward people for raw volume you may be encouraging poor or even terrible behaviors—surgeons ignoring the very sick to operate on easier, faster cases, internists similarly aiming for simpler, younger patients, rather than those with multiple medical problems with very complicated management issues. If you only measure how quickly someone loads data into an EMR, you may be discouraging them from spending time to talk with a patient, from doing a thorough physical examination, or from talking with family members or trusted colleagues. All of those are important things that smart professionals know is part of their job. Make sure that you are encouraging the right behaviors from your professionals and not just focusing on a small, easily measured metric. You want them to do a hard job—being a nurse, a physician, etc.—and you should want them to do it well. These are complicated roles and oversimplifying them will frustrate your group and worse can lead to stupid or even dangerous outcomes.

In the world of healthcare academics, this conundrum of misplaced incentives has implications for the core mission of the institution. Traditionally, this has rested on a triad of clinical care, teaching, and research. While not all institutions of learning are equally good at all three, all of them profess to encourage these three intertwined but separate goals. If you only reward your professors on the basis of their clinical activity, you shouldn't be surprised that the other two parts of the triad dwindle. They are only human, but they are also smart humans and there are several potential outcomes, none of them ideal. First, they may move on to an institution that is more in line with the ethos of that of a traditional medical school. Second, they will stay and try to work overtime to make it all work but likely become burned out. Lastly, you may literally get what you pay for and watch as everything except their clinical work withers.

*Image credit: President Kennedy and Vice President Johnson prior to the introduction ceremony for the Workmens' Compensation Commemorative Stamp in Wisconsin, 31 August 1961, by Abbie Rowe*

# 28

# Succession Leadership

*"I used to believe in forever, but forever is too good to be true."*
—*Alan Alexander Milne in* Winnie the Pooh, *1882–1956*

## INTRODUCTION

One of the hardest decisions for successful leaders is deciding when to step down. Many leaders find it very hard to leave. Some, like Teddy Roosevelt, leave and then find it impossible to stay away, which then creates problems for their successor. This leads to the commonly given advice to presidents, CEOs, and other leaders to try for a clean break. The problem in many situations of that approach is that there is often far too little planning and preparation for that break, leading to a vacuum and discontinuity in leadership when the end of your service comes. In 2010, at major leadership meeting in my field, a survey of the leaders in attendance revealed that less than half of the practices represented had a plan for succession. I have been looking at this ever since and it doesn't seem to be improving. This chapter will focus on ways that you can help prepare the next leader for the challenges that she or he faces.

## STRATEGIC PLANNING FOR LEADERSHIP TRANSITIONS

The first point about succession is that it is inevitable. Like death and taxes, it is one of the few sure things in your life. You will not work forever nor will you lead forever so you need to consider ways that you can help your group prepare for that day. An added benefit of actively planning for and preparing for that day is that it will also help in the unfortunate circumstance if your reign ends prematurely. Not to be morbid about this,

Leadership Lessons for Health Care Providers. http://dx.doi.org/10.1016/B978-0-12-801866-8.00028-7

but if one person is doing most of the leadership work in a medium sized practice while everyone else focuses on clinical work and no one else has been involved in leadership or prepared for a leadership role (or even briefed on the major issues), then that practice is always one car accident or airplane crash away from a leadership crisis with both short- and long-term implications for the group's success. To the extent that your succession planning begins early, it can help with this potential problem as well.

## TACTICAL STEPS IN SUCCESSION PLANNING

### Start to Think About a Date

In an ideal situation, you should start your tenure by planning and working with the end in mind. That includes thinking about how you hand the reigns over to your successor. As we saw previously, the majority of leaders in my field do not have a plan and that may also be as bad or even worse in your part of the healthcare world. Most leaders do not begin thinking about this until their age or their personal circumstances force them to confront the issue. I advise leaders to start preparing at least 5 years ahead of their expected date of retirement. This is usually more of a window (plus or minus a few years) than a date, but it is a big step forward in getting the process underway.

### Gain Buy-In From Your Group or Organization

As the time gets closer and you begin to focus on the reality of succession, you need to have a serious discussion about the transition with the members of your group or institution. At this point, you need their support with your decision to begin the planning process and discussion. Many leaders loathe to take this step because they are concerned that this will alarm the group and cause anxiety. In some groups that may occur, but it is much more likely that the group members have been thinking about this almost as much or more than you have, so if anything they will be relieved that someone has finally brought up this delicate issue at your partners meeting.

## DELEGATE AND DISTRIBUTE

The aforementioned header is good, general advice for most leaders, but as we have discussed in the section on delegation, far too rare in our fields until you get into the larger practices. Asking one person to shoulder all of the leadership tasks is a poor way to run an organization and carries the risks as outlined previously. If your group is run this way now, then thinking about succession is a good reason to start to distribute some of the leadership work among a select group of individuals. It is also the next step in your succession plan.

This accomplishes several worthy goals at once. First, it helps to train promising candidates for leadership work. Second, it establishes a more robust structure for the organization that starts helping you know and will also be part of your legacy. Third, it allows you to watch these candidates and assess their capability for replacing you. It may sound obvious, but the best test of a leader is to have them lead. By starting to distribute leadership tasks to likely candidates, you can test your potential replacements. Many medical practices today are likely to promote from within to fill an important leadership vacancy, rather than bring someone in from outside. If this is your expectation, then these three steps are the way to embark.

## EVALUATE

If you are planning on promoting from within your group be wary of skipping any of the aforementioned steps or of moving through them too quickly. It is critical that you spend time evaluating your possible successors and the best way to evaluate their leadership skills is by giving them leadership opportunities. Sometimes the person in your group who seemed to be an obvious choice for a leader turns out to be mediocre once you give them some leadership tasks. By starting at least a few years in advance and by giving people incremental amounts of responsibility you will have a chance to assess whether they are right people to carry the group forward. Getting outside help from a smart consultant may be helpful at this stage. They can take a fresh look at the candidates and their performance. They won't have the emotional and historical baggage with these people that may cloud your judgement. In the end it is your call, but as in other domains it doesn't hurt a leader to have some additional expertise and advice in a difficult situation.

## MENTOR

Mentoring is critical to developing your next generation of leaders. This involves both general principles of leadership as well as the key practice specific information that you have accumulated during your tenure. Don't just throw your candidates into leadership challenges, mentor them as they grow into their responsibilities. Contrary to conventional mythology, leaders are not born. Most other types of important organizations use mentoring in order to develop their leaders and you as a leader need to mentor your future leaders. You have an important responsibility here, particularly for the specifics, but you should also use external resources as well. You should consider sending them to courses on leadership and perhaps more formal certificate or degree granting programs so that they can gain additional skills and insights into the tasks and roles of being a leader.

## CONSIDER YOUR PERSONAL PLAN

Most of the aforementioned milestones are focused on the greater good of your group and the plan for the group and the future leader. You also need to consider your personal needs. Are you going to retire when you step down or are you going to continue to be a member of the group? Are you staying in the community or are you moving to another state to start your retirement? Think carefully about this. After a long tenure as the leader, will you be happy as a partner while someone else leads? Will you be able to step aside? Will you need to retire entirely from the practice in order to keep yourself from meddling in the current leader's work. Your replacement will probably always be able to benefit from your advice, but if you are unable to completely hand over the reigns, you may make it impossible for them to do their jobs and you may make yourself look foolish. Think of the example of Teddy Roosevelt who embarrassed himself and damaged his party so much that the election split between him and his immediate successor, Taft, meant that the opposition party won the White House. If that doesn't have enough impact, then think of the numerous examples of professional athletes who kept coming back long after their prime, embarrassing themselves, but unable to resist the lure of returning until they got hurt and/or humiliated themselves.

Try instead to aim for what people like Johnny Carson and Jerry Seinfeld succeeded in doing—go out on top and really go. That isn't easy for successful leaders. Alpha leaders have great experience, and in the process of gaining that experience, their identity and self-esteem become tied up in the position. That can make it hard, very hard, to let go. Leaving before someone forces you to can be a very difficult decision to make and for some leaders even more difficult to carry out. Have the courage to go at the right time rather than waiting until someone has to gently tell you that that time is long past.

In your case, begin the planning and consider the aforementioned milestones to help making this difficult procvess both less painful and more successful.

## KEY POINTS

1. Succession planning begins with you and should begin now.
2. Timing is important—try to go out on top.
3. While every plan will be different, there are several key milestones that you need to meet in order to smooth the transition.
4. You and your group need to work together to make this work.
5. Both mentoring and formal preparation are keys to leadership development.
6. Selecting a successor should occur after a process of progressive delegation and evaluation to make sure that you have the right person with the right preparation.

*Image credit: The Oval Office in 1981, during the first year of Reagan Presidency; Wikimedia Commons*

# Leadership: The Last 100 Days

*"This is the end, my only friend, the end*
*Of our elaborate plans, the end*
*Of everything that stands, the end..."*
—**Jim Morrison, lead singer of The Doors, in the song**
**"The End", 1943-1971**

## INTRODUCTION

Leadership is a play in several acts. The final act is important in itself but if you start thinking about from time to time early in your career it may also act as a guide to how to conduct yourself during the other portions of your career. This chapter provides insights into how the inevitability of the finiteness of leadership need not be a cause for despair, but instead a motivator to make your mark as a leader while you have your moment on the stage. The discussion closes with a suggestion from the history of the US presidency on how to close out your time as a leader with a gesture that perhaps will be a helping hand to the woman or man who follows you.

## COMING TO THE END: DEEP THOUGHTS

Like many things that matter deeply to us, leadership is a difficult and at times contentious topic. This is also true when we contemplate how to plan for the end of leadership. I hope that this is not too depressing a topic, but it is an important one that we need to face. I also hope that when you are down to your final 3 months or so, you will have already followed the advice about succession leadership which will put you in good stead as you wind down. Also, remember that as we have discussed throughout

**Leadership Lessons for Health Care Providers.** http://dx.doi.org/10.1016/B978-0-12-801866-8.00029-9

the book, one of the keys to success is to begin with the end in mind in order to guide you in working toward your goals.

In the mid 2000s, I used to do a CME program on economic and financial issues for health professionals. In the program, I included a speaker on estate planning since that was a topic that many of our attendees felt they needed to learn more about for themselves. The notion that many healthcare professionals are too busy to pay sufficient attention to important financial matters certainly seems to be true for many of the physicians in my generation and the one older than mine. This is obviously a difficult topic, people don't like to contemplate their own mortality and this had the potential to be the low point of the course. Fortunately, the speaker had a great sense of humor despite the grim topic of his work. One of his best lines was related to an anecdote about his clients who would open their discussions with him by saying "this is what I would like to do with my estate if I die." He would gently remind them that for all of us the end is not a matter of "if" but rather of other questions such as "how" or perhaps "when." Unfortunately, barring great leaps forward in technology, for all of us "if" is not part of the discussion, it is an inevitability. In the case of your leadership work, it also not a matter of "if I step down" or "if I have to stop." One way or another your time of leadership will come to an end so the real questions revolve around: when, why and how, not "if."

However, this is not only a chapter for those who are at the end of their careers so don't skip it if you are more than 5 years away at this point. Rather, it is for everyone who will spend their careers in leadership tasks and roles. As we close out this chapter, we will focus on ways to think about the end of your leadership role. The deeper insight is that this isn't something that you start thinking about when you are 5 years away from retirement. Rather this thinking should affect what you are doing now and for years and even decades before that day of retirement finally does arrive. As Stephen Covey put it succinctly in his book, *The 7 habits of highly successful people* (1989): begin with the end in mind.

In the chapter on succession, we focused on the process of preparing your group and the new leader for the changeover. That section discussed the tactical and other practical aspects of handing the reins of power over to a successor. Here we will focus on the personal issues for you and combine two analogies that I would like you to consider as you ponder your leadership career.

## BEGINNING WITH THE END IN MIND

The first is an exercise that I initially encountered in college that is popular with management consulting types as well as career coaches: try to write your obituary today. This focuses the mind, albeit a bit morbidly, on the question of what you would like to have accomplished when the chance to accomplish is over. This is far more than a "bucket list" of things to do before you are dead, but instead is chance to explore how you would like to be remembered—what are the big things that matter to you in life. It probably isn't drinking the 100 most expensive wines on the planet, it is rather the more personal issues of how you will be remembered by family and friends and what your career meant. Taking it a step further, it should delve into an exploration of what you doing now and how that interfaces with the goals that you have embedded in the obituary. The deeper purpose of the project should be to do more than just ask what you think are worthy endeavors for this life, but go further and ask if your daily activities align with this. Are you doing the things that matter most to you? Are you living today in a manner that will lead you there? If your goals don't fit your life then which will you alter: the goals or your life?

## LETTERS FOR YOURSELF AND YOUR SUCCESSOR

The second inspiration for the project in this chapter is something that we touched on previously in this book—the tradition of an outgoing US president leaving a letter in the Oval office to their successor. Only a few verified copies are readily available and not all are profound in their wisdom, but it is nevertheless a touching tradition, particularly in the politically polarized times that characterize the period when the first edition of this book was written. Often the notes are being left for bitter rivals, in some cases even for someone who just defeated you in a rough election, yet they are positive and encouraging in their advice. In one that I read recently, there was a touching note of good sportsmanship. In this penultimate chapter, my advice to you is to consider writing your letter to your successor now, rather than the night before you leave. Starting now will be analogous to the obituary exercise—it will help you and will in fact help you now. Incorporate elements of the obituary that refer to you career and specifically those of your tenure in leadership—what you hope to have accomplished and how you would like your tenure to be remembered, but focus on the issues of success in your leadership role. Here are some questions that can help you get started on this:

1. The toughest thing for me at the beginning was…
2. When I was your age, I wish that I had known …
3. My greatest accomplishments were…
4. I have done the following things to help prepare you for this position…
5. The key people who can help you are…
6. The most important key to success in this place is…

7. When the going is rough, remember…
8. Going forward, you should consider doing the following things to help you succeed…

---

## KEY POINTS

1. Use planning and strategy in your leadership work right up to the end.
2. Plan your legacy.
3. Extend a helping hand to your successor.
4. Consider the questions in this chapter before you get to the end to help both yourself and the person who inherits your responsibilities.
5. Helping the next person to be a leader will also help your legacy, but also you work now if you start today.

*Image credit: Stairway to the light. First step © Antonov Roman/shutterstock*

# 30

# Conclusions and Next Steps

One of my frustrations with some of the books that I read during my MBA program was that they told interesting business stories and made for good reads but it wasn't clear how to implement what was in the book. In particular, they rarely included advice on what you should do next. This final chapter is included here to help with that transition. In the end, you will find your own way and I hope that the previous chapters have given you ideas in how you might become a better leader in your medical work. As we close this book, I wanted to give you some additional suggestions to help you move forward. Here are some next steps that can help you implement what we have discussed and help you step beyond what we covered here.

## STEP 1: NEVER STOP LEARNING ABOUT LEADERSHIP

Smart leaders know that they need to keep learning. They need to stay sharp and they also need to develop new skills in order to stay ahead of the competition. This is particularly true in healthcare where we have the twin challenges of rapid changes in medical technology coupled with the economic, political, and societal challenges that are changing our work landscape. Go back and take another look through the curriculum that we covered and ask yourself what you know, what you don't know, what you need to review, and what you need to know more about. As you put together a personal learning program, try a variety of modalities in how you learn. Mix up face to face classes with books, lectures, and online opportunities. You need depth in these areas, so beware of a product that claims it can teach you advanced finance in ten easy lessons—good luck with that, it takes more than ten lessons and some of them are not that easy. You also need material that is up to date. A book about managing hospitals in the Reagan era

Leadership Lessons for Health Care Providers. http://dx.doi.org/10.1016/B978-0-12-801866-8.00030-5

would make for interesting historical reading, but you as a leader need information that it as current as possible. We live in a time when changes from the Centers for Medicare and Medicaid Services are both significant for our practices in healthcare and are the norm. Things change regularly and often have substantial impacts in how we are regulated, how we are paid, and which procedures and tools we can use in certain circumstances.

## STEP 2: LEARN ABOUT OTHER LEADERS AND LEARN FROM THEM

One of the fun things that I have been able to do in my career is to meet and talk with leaders. One of the questions that I ask is what books do you read (or if they answer that they are too busy—what would you read if you could). An interesting answer that comes up a lot from prominent leaders is that they read a lot of biography. They like to read about other leaders both current and historical. Sometimes they are reading about their own mentors or their own competitors. Many of them are very interested in history and the challenges that other leaders have faced at critical moments. You should look into this genre. In general, I have been a pretty avid reader in my life, but I have to admit that until I went to business school, I didn't have much interest myself in biography as a genre. I thought that a lot of it was boring and at times self-serving. That changed with being assigned several good business biographies as class assignments. Give this a try yourself. It is refreshing to read about a famous leader who you think walked on water and find out that they made many of the same mistakes that you have made. Remember what we discussed about the battles that Washington lost. People forget about that because of the important ones that he won. Most people forget the important election that Lincoln didn't win or the personal problems and challenges that he faced. Like the Beatles being called an overnight sensation after they put in years of hard work in the UK and Germany or the genius Edison finding lots of ways to not invent a light bulb before he finally found a way that worked, we can take comfort in knowing that other people have struggled to succeed too. If our notions about success in other people are limited magical thinking rather than a more realistic view, then we may give up when our own experiences also include setbacks and failures. You may also pick up tips in how people have handled difficult situations, how they have handled difficult people and changed themselves and their organizations in difficult times. Learning from great leaders can be a great help to you in your work.

# STEP 3: GET THE BEST INTELLIGENCE YOU CAN

Another thing that I have picked up from great leaders is that they pay very close attention to the world around them. They are up to date on current political, economic, social, and scientific trends. They not only pay attention to the news, they strive to get an understanding of what is going on behind the scenes. Like those who have to make difficult military decisions, they know that their success will depend upon having superior intel compared to their opponents. Since much of the basic news is often colored by political spin and the need to sell products and/or ideas, don't rely just on the most popular television, radio, or web sources. Reliability should trump popularity in your choices. Also given the polarization that dominates US media, diligently try to understand current events from more than one point in the political spectrum. Both extremes may be biased and less than truthful, but contrasting them can help you find the truth that lies somewhere in the middle of spectrum or perhaps elsewhere. A helpful tip here is to occasionally get your news from a source outside your home country. Understanding how others see events will help broaden your perspective and you may learn quite a bit. One of the reasons that I read the Economist is that is written from an editorial perspective outside the United States and thus gives a very different view of events around the world (and in the United States) than I can find from US domestic based news sources.

Go for depth in how you keep yourself informed. For science, try to use a respected scientific source rather than a general newspaper. For economics and finance, use sources that provide detailed commentary and information, rather than the babble on the local radio about why the stock market went up and down. That is not only uniformative, it is often misleading, that is, the stock market went up at 11:00 am due to an event and when it went down at 3:00 pm they blame it on the same event or phenomena. One of the things that I look for in sources is similar to how I think about medical tests: how well do they diagnose or predict the future? Did this website give me insights into what would happen in east Asia or with the stock market or in a domestic election? Were they just trying to spin the news or push a political agenda or did they provide good data and analysis that had predictive heft?

# STEP 4: BE AMBITIOUS

The world needs talented, ethical leaders. If you are a good leader, aim high. For some of us in healthcare, we are really only thinking about becoming a leader to rise to the top of our local group, department, or perhaps the institution. We enjoy healthcare despite its challenges and we would like to stay in healthcare. Let me repeat for emphasis: if you can and are willing do aim high or higher. Be the best leader you can at every level you reach, but don't be afraid to keep going up. If you channel your amibition well, having determination to look above and beyond will make you better at your current level even if you don't progress beyond it. You will understand how the people above you in the organization think and it will help you perform at your current level.

## STEP 5: SEEK OUT THE COMPANY OF OTHER LEADERS

All of us in the healthcare field have meetings. Many of these are scientific and educational— allowing us to keep up with new information in our fields and to review material when we are getting rusty. As leaders you should also seek out meetings where you can meet and network with other leaders. Don't just seek out people at your level. Try to meet people with more experience and responsibility so that you can learn from them. Also, don't just associate with people like yourself, for example, if you are surgeon try to understand what nursing leaders are doing. Conversely if you are nurse. At times you may want to really push the envelope and meet with leaders in other industries. They have interesting solutions in their work that you can often adapt and apply in yours. Lastly, don't shy away from spending time with people in government, both civil service and politicians. Some of us in science and medical are disconnected from the political process. Politicians at times have been quite unkind to healthcare professionals. However, healthcare is large portion of the US economy. It is simply too important to all of us. If you are reading this book and are a US healthcare professional you are probably also a taxpayer, a purchaser of medical services. You may have relied on the Medicare system for your parent's care and you may have children who will have to grow up in the nation that we leave behind. Healthcare is not only a cost. It is an extraordinary economic engine that creates valuable exports. It also is a huge sector that employs a large number of people and in many towns, the biggest employer now is no longer a factory, it is a hospital or other healthcare entity, such as a health insurance company. Understanding how politicians and other government leaders are thinking about healthcare and in turn giving them your insights as a healthcare leader can be mutually beneficial.

By doing these things now, you will steer a better leadership course in these difficult times and you will better align your day to day efforts with your big goals (and vice versa). Finally, when you come to the end of your leadership journey, I hope that you will be proud of your time as a leader and I hope that these pages will have helped you on your quest. So we have come to the end of this book. Hopefully for you it is rather the beginning of the next steps and perhaps the end of the beginning. Our health system needs your leadership. Best of luck in your tenure as a leader.

All the best,
Frank

# Bibliography

Brus-Ramer M, Lexa FJ, Kassing P, McGinty G. (in press). International perspectives on radiology in preventive screening. *J. Am. Coll. Radiol.*

Collins J. *Good to Great: Why Some Companies Make the Leap... and Others Don't.* New York, NY: Harper Collins; 2001.

Collins J, Hansen MT. *Great by Choice: Uncertainty, Chaos, and Luck—Why Some Thrive Despite Them All.* New York, NY: Harper Collins; 2011.

Covey SR. *The 7 Habits of Highly Effective People: Powerful Lessons in Personal Change.* New York, NY: Simon & Schuster; 1989.

Covey SR. *Principle-Centered Leadership.* New York, NY: Simon & Schuster; 1991.

Drucker PF. *The Essential Drucker: The Best of Sixty Years of Peter Drucker's Essential Writings on Management.* New York, NY: Collins Business Essentials, Harper Collins; 2001.

Drucker PF. The American CEO. The Wall Street Journal, December 30; 2004. Available from: http://www.wsj.com/articles/SB110436476581112426

Enzmann DR, Beauchamp Jr NJ, Norbash A. Scenario planning. *J. Am. Coll. Radiol.* 2011;**8**(3):175–9.

Fallows J. The passionless presidency: the trouble with Jimmy Carter's administration. *The Atlantic Monthly;* 1979. Available from: http://www.theatlantic.com/magazine/archive/1979/05/the-passionless-presidency/308516/

Fisher R, Sharp A. *Getting It Done: How to Lead When You're Not in Charge.* New York, NY: Harper Business; 1998.

Gill IE, Ondategui-Parra S, Nathanson E, Seiferth J, Ros PR. Strategic planning in radiology. *J. Am. Coll. Radiol.* 2005;**2**(4):348–57.

Hofstede G. The cultural relativity of organizational practices and theories. *J. Int. Bus. Stud.* 1983;**14**(2):75–89.

Hurley R. Trust me. *The Wall Street Journal R4,* October 24; 2011.

Iglehart JK. Health insurers and medical-imaging policy—a work in progress. *N. Engl. J. Med.* 2009;**360**(10):1030–7.

Imai M. *Kaizen: The Key to Japan's Competitive Success.* New York, NY: Random House; 1986.

Jacob S. Facing an uncertain future, physicians increasingly throw in the towel. *Healthcare magazine,* Dallas, TX; 2014. Available from: http://healthcare.dmagazine.com/2014/08/27/facing-an-uncertain-future-physiciansthrow-in-the-towel

Jha S, Lexa F. Wicked problems. *J. Am. Coll. Radiol.* 2014;**11**(5):437–9.

Lexa FJ. 300,000,000 customers: patient perspectives on service and quality. *J. Am. Coll. Radiol.* 2006;**3**(5):346–50.

Lexa FJ. Advanced marketing: how to protect and advance your practice. *J. Am. Coll. Radiol.* 2007;**4**(2):119–24.

Lexa FJ. Qualities of great leadership. *J. Am. Coll. Radiol.* 2008;**5**(4):598–9.

Lexa FJ. Delegation: getting it right to lead successfully. *J. Am. Coll. Radiol.* 2008;**5**(7):850–2.

Lexa FJ. Making the grade: levels of leadership, part 1. *J. Am. Coll. Radiol.* 2009;**6**(1):12–3.

Lexa FJ. Making the grade: levels of leadership, part 2. *J. Am. Coll. Radiol.* 2009;**6**(4):228–9.

Lexa FJ. Leadership: style and structures. *J. Am. Coll. Radiol.* 2010;**7**(4):301–3.

Lexa FJ. Principled leadership. *J. Am. Coll. Radiol.* 2010;**7**(7):529–30.

Lexa FJ. Educating leaders: a foundation curriculum for radiologists. *J. Am. Coll. Radiol.* 2011;**8**(7):517.

**Leadership Lessons for Health Care Providers.** http://dx.doi.org/10.1016/B978-0-12-801866-8.00038-X

Lexa FJ, Chan SC. Scenario analysis and strategic planning: practical applications for radiology practices. *J. Am. Coll. Radiol.* 2010;**7**(5):369–73.

Muroff LR. Implementing an effective organization and governance structure for a radiology practice. *J. Am. Coll. Radiol.* 2004;**1**(1):26–32.

Neff TJ, Citrin JM. *You're in Charge—Now What?: The 8 Point Plan.* New York, NY: Crown Business; 2005.

Pink DH. *Drive: The Surprising Truth About What Motivates Us.* New York, NY: Riverhead Books; 2011.

Shenk JW. *Powers of Two: Finding the Essence of Innovation in Creative Pairs.* Boston, MA: Houghton Mifflin Harcourt; 2014.

Tavris C, Aronson E. *Mistakes Were Made (But Not by Me): Why We Justify Foolish Beliefs, Bad Decisions, and Hurtful Acts.* Boston, MA: Houghton Mifflin Harcourt; 2007.

The Economist. Mao and the art of management: a role model, of sorts. *The Economist,* December 19; 2007. Available from: http://www.economist.com/node/10311230

Watkins M. *The First 90 Days: Critical Success Strategies for New Leaders at All Levels.* Boston, MA: Harvard Business School Press; 2003.

Weiss RP. Crisis leadership: since September 11, business leaders have been reassessing how well prepared they are to lead (lead on!). *Talent Dev.* 2002;**56**(3) 28+.

White C. FDR and the unfinished agenda. Part IV: the first 100 days. *ePluribus Media;* 2006. Available from: http://www.epluribusmedia.org/features/2006/200609_FDR_pt4.html

# Index

## A

Abilities, 6, 73, 89, 144
Academic healthcare practices, 23
Accountability, 48, 55, 88
Activities, 98
Administration, 24, 114
  hospital, 96, 164
  presidential, 24, 54, 132
Admonition, 34
Adulation, 46
Advisors, 28, 54, 108
  legal, 114
Africa, 3
Agendas, 24, 47, 171
  active, 24
  domestic, 114
  for goals, 38
  and implement it aggressively, 27
  keep asking yourself about, 27
Aggressive goals, 42
Agreement, 25
Agriculture, 10
Alignment, 168
Alliances, 162–163
Ambiguity, 75
American business, 19
American College of Radiology has a
    Commission on Leadership and
    Practice Developmen, 67
Ambition, 199
Anger, 83, 112
Angry, 112
Antagonism, 18
Architecture of knowledge worker's office
    space, 81
Assessment, 53, 162
Atrocities, 46
Attention, 34, 37, 38, 92, 175, 199
  diverting, 91
Attention deficit/hyperactivity disorder, 103
Authoritarian organizations, 81
Authoritarian style, 82
Automobile factory, 180
Autonomy, 51

## B

Bad situation, things that do after this
    happens. *See also* Failures; Mistake
Balancing responsibilities, 95
Basketball game, 10
Behavioral trait, 3
Behaviors, 48, 114
  adverse, 42
  bad, 112, 173
  management, 17
  punish negative, 43
  terrible, 182
  trait, 3
  unprincipled, 47
"Benign" dictatorship, 82
Bike helmets, 5
Blind spots, 80
  problem, overcoming, 132
Budgets, 96
Building network, 77
Build team, 28
  of capable people you trust, 36
Bush, George W., 114
Business, 3, 17, 18, 45, 77
  leaders, 19, 45, 89
  literature, success factors in, 28
  management, 46
  meetings, 6
  newspaper, 19
  person, 113
  press, 18
  school classroom teaching, 74

## C

Cabinet secretaries, 28
Cable news, 45
Campaign, 24
Cardiac intensive care unit, 4
Carter, Jimmy, 53
  challenges, 54
  delegation, 53
  management style, 53
  meticulous attention and ability, 53
Catastrophe, 156